MW00615359

NAVIGATING
Diversity

IN OUR MOST SEGREGATED HOUR

DAN BERRY

Copyright © 2020 by Dan Berry

Navigating Diversity: In Our Most Segregated Hour

All rights reserved. No part of this publication may be reproduced, distributed or transmitted in any form or by any means, including photocopying, recording, or other electronic or mechanical methods, without the prior written permission of the publisher, except in the case of brief quotations embodied in critical reviews and certain other noncommercial uses permitted by copyright law.

Although the author and publisher have made every effort to ensure that the information in this book was correct at press time, the author and publisher do not assume and hereby disclaim any liability to any party for any loss, damage, or disruption caused by errors or omissions, whether such errors or omissions result from negligence, accident, or any other cause.

Adherence to all applicable laws and regulations, including international, federal, state and local governing professional licensing, business practices, advertising, and all other aspects of doing business in the US, Canada or any other jurisdiction is the sole responsibility of the reader and consumer.

Neither the author nor the publisher assumes any responsibility or liability whatsoever on behalf of the consumer or reader of this material. Any per-ceived slight of any individual or organization is purely unintentional.

The resources in this book are provided for informational purposes only and should not be used to replace the specialized training and professional judgment of a health care or mental health care professional.

Neither the author nor the publisher can be held responsible for the use of the information provided within this book. Please always consult a trained professional before making any decision regarding treatment of yourself or others.

Scriptures in the book were from the following:

Scripture taken from the New King James Version. Copyright © 1979, 1980, 1982 by Thomas Nelson, Inc. Used by permission. All rights reserved.

Scripture taken from The Voice Version. Copyright © 2012 by Thomas Nelson, Inc. Used by permission.

Scripture taken from the Amplified Bible, Copyright © 1954, 1958, 1962, 1964, 1965, 1987 by The Lockman Foundation. Used by permission.

Scripture quotations taken from the Holy Bible, New Living Translation, Copyright © 1996, 2004. Used by permission of Tyndale House Publishers, Inc. Wheaton, Illinois 60189. All rights reserved.

All scripture quotations in the publication are from The Message. Copyright © by Eugene H. Peterson 1993, 1994, 1995, 1996, 2000, 2001, 2002. Used by permission of NavPress Publishing Group.

ISBN: 978-0-578-67807-8
Library of Congress Control Number: 2019912330
Printed in the United States of America

Download the free "Heart Preparation Guide."

Go to: www.bridgebuildingsolutions.com

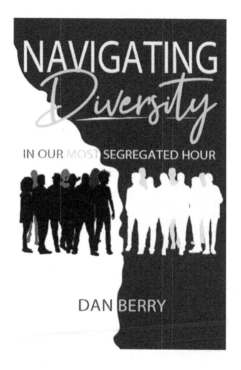

Answering the Reflective Questions will encourage
your self-examination.

It takes an open, teachable heart to not only start this journey
but to stay committed to being a true repairer of the breach. We
cannot move forward until we first know where we are.

Please take your time as you honestly reflect where you are and
what the real issues that keep us divided are.

Dedication

This book is dedicated to the hidden beam of my life, Anne Marie Leonhart Berry. She has been my partner in life and ministry for over 44 years. Without her support, her unwavering confidence, and belief in me, this journey would never have been realized.

With special gratitude to Dr. Lucretia Carter Berry, who helped me see more clearly and help me understand how important my story was to tell.

Finally, this book is dedicated to the Lord Jesus Christ and the people of Cornerstone Family Church. For years you have embraced this vision to bring people together from all walks of life. Without you, my ever so faithful bridgebuilders, we couldn't have come this far.

Table of Contents

Foreword

I wept as I read chapter seven. I was overwhelmed by a spirit of healing so nurturing that it decalcified trauma firmly affixed to my soul and overtook me with tidal waves of joy and hope —the impact expressed through tears. As tears streamed down my cheeks, my grin widened to an optimistic smile.

Isn't that how healing happens? First, we acknowledge the wound. Then, we rush to stop the pain. Next, we allow the wound to heal and repair. Finally, the repaired wound is healed and STRONG.

As the church, we know this. We also acknowledge and teach the restorative power of the great I AM, in whose image we are made. We also know that according to Jesus' final prayer, our humanity has been established as one with each other and one with I AM. So, why is the American church known for passively aligning with divisive, dehumanizing, racist beliefs, policies, politics, and practices? Why aren't we known for powerfully resisting the race lie and racism? Why are we not known for oneness?

Ours is a young nation. And in its infancy, the American Church can boast of its religious influence on shaping America's consciousness. However, we do not hold a formidable record for leading the deep, hard, extended work of healing our nation from the destructive race construct. Instead, we fester in the chronic wounds of race/ism.

But, as evidenced by Pastor Dan Berry's story, all is not lost. The church is a living entity. We are endowed with resilience! Through hope's lens, I see, clearly, that Pastor Dan's journey — the one he has vulnerably shared in these pages — has marked the path for white-American, Evangelical pastors who are hearing the clarion call to rise up and lead our nation to heal from race/ism.

Through Pastor Dan's story, those of us who have been far from the work of antiracism will see a way to it. We will understand the urgency for the deep transformative work required to unleash healing and repair. We will recognize this work as love. We will understand that love is hard work, but it's our work. And though we may read about his pitfalls and get nervous about the challenges we face, we will be encouraged by his growth to keep pressing towards liberty.

Pastor Dan is my father-in-law. I am honored to have witnessed his transformation from a lead pastor satisfied with his diverse church in Iowa to a student and agent of antiracism repair work serving beyond his state of Iowa.

He doesn't know this, but long before he penned these chapters, I was sharing his journey with friends — friends who need hope — friends who need to know that white Evangelical pastors, dads, moms, brothers, and sisters can and will do this hard work of love.

Dr. Lucretia Carter Berry, daughter-in-law
Author of *What LIES Between Us, Fostering First Steps Toward Racial Healing* Journal & Guide
Founder of *Brownicity- Many Hues One Humanity*

x

Introduction

I am the oldest of four kids. My younger siblings were all sisters. As we grew, there was a lot of fighting amongst us. We drove our parents crazy with our constant bickering. My sister Denise and I were the oldest, and with four years between us and the younger two, I remember how we would manipulate them into choosing sides. We knew it made our parents mad, but we didn't even give it a thought concerning how painful it might be to them.

Thankfully, as we got older, the bickering went away. But I know from Pastoring for 40 plus years that some families never recover. Sometimes people can't wait to leave. Some just drift apart with very little relationship between them.

Could it be that this is what has happened in the Body of Christ?

Have centuries of bickering caused us to drift apart? Has thinking that our theology is closer to the truth than anyone else's caused us to allow gulfs of division to separate us.

Did our fighting over belief systems cause us to even participate in and uphold the race construct? Did it cause us to miss the evil of this in our sacred places? Did it lead the church to choose the wrong side?

For whatever reason, we find the American church hour on Sunday mornings to be the most segregated hour of the week.

In my journey, I have become keenly aware of how much this grieves the heart of our Father God. He longs for His kids to stop the nonsense and begin to treat each other with the love and dignity He expects.

Could it be that our relationship with one another is as important to God as our relationship with Him?

I believe so, and let me give you a couple of reasons.

First of all, when Jesus was confronted with the question about what was the most important commandment, His answer was as follows:

Matthew 22:37-40 (NLT)

[37] Jesus replied, "' You must love the Lord your God with all your heart, all your soul, and all your mind.' [38] This is the first and greatest commandment. [39] A second is equally important: 'Love your neighbor as yourself.' [40] The entire law and all the demands of the prophets are based on these two commandments."

When He said that the 'love your neighbor as yourself' commandment was as important to Him as the 'love Him with all of my heart' commandment. That got my attention, and it changed my heart.

But I have to say that the last verse, where He said that the entire law and all the demands of the prophets are based on the two most important commandments, rocked my world!

If I didn't get these two commandments, nothing else I believed mattered. Think about that. The second reason is this.

In Jesus' final prayer in John 17, He prayed for us. He desired that we would find oneness with one another and with Him.

I have to believe that if our hearts are really after His before He returns, we will find ourselves immersed in a desire to be a part of the healing that needs to take place. We will come out of the shadows of complacency and find ourselves desiring to heal the divisions that are so prevalent among us.

It's my prayer that this story will not only help you take those first steps but will also help you find the courage you will need to take on and dismantle these century-old strongholds.

This is journey is personal, and there will be a cost. But we need to do our part to eliminate the reputation of being the most segregated hour.

"Love recognizes no barriers.
It jumps hurdles, leaps fences,
Penetrates walls to arrive at
its destination full of hope."

Maya Angelou

1

The Journey Begins...

Whenever you get ready to go somewhere, run an errand, go to the grocery store, go on a vacation, or even a mission's trip, you know the destination and, with the help of google maps, the route to get there.

You make your lists and plan out what you are going to do when you get there long before you ever begin. The preparation can be as important as the journey.

With God, it's not always like that. Sometimes it's just a simple "go." Have you ever said yes to God, thinking you knew where he was taking you only to find out later, you were wrong? We are not saying that there isn't planning and preparation for the places he takes us and the things that he wants us to do, but it's not always that visible. We don't frequently know the end from the beginning.

In ministry, I have hoped that my ideas and my plans were His, but I have to say it wasn't always the case.

Proverbs 19:21 (NLT)

21 You can make many plans,
but the Lord's purpose will prevail.

When I was young, we left Des Moines, and my family moved to an acreage north of a small town. I took little notice of the fact it was an all-white community. When you are immersed in whiteness, you don't think about being white. Growing up in this community was wonderful but lacked any ethnic or cultural experience.

Sports became a big part of my life growing up, which brought a shallow sense of fulfillment to my heart. My wife Anne tells everyone that I grew up in a lifestyle like the fictional "Pollyanna," story a beautiful, stable family who loved and supported each other.

I have to mention that as good as my childhood was, we didn't know anything about God. I can only remember a few times that we went to church. It wasn't that we didn't believe in God; we just didn't know him.

Sports led me to think about the possibility of attending college. The idea that I could be the first one in my family to go to college made me dream about the possibility of doing something with my life. I remember wondering if God had some sense of purpose for my life. As confusing as the whole God thing was to me, deep down, I knew I was here for a reason.

Academics was not my strong suit, yet somehow, I got into college and did end up graduating with a Business Degree. In addition to a degree, a couple of pretty important things happened in those four years. First of all, I met the love of my life, Anne, and we were married at the end of my sophomore year. What were we thinking?

Secondly, we both gave our lives to Christ a year after we were married. With one year of school left to complete, we found ourselves immersed in a great church with many other young couples that were trying to find their way in this new life Jesus had introduced us to. We couldn't get enough of God. Serving Him in our church is what we began to live for. School almost became secondary. But I was too close to the end to give up, and I aspired to work for a large company and someday own my own business and serve in our church.

After graduating with a business degree, I was able to land a great job in a worldwide agricultural firm that was headquartered here in Des Moines. Our lives took off. We were able to buy our first home, had a couple of babies, and were living the dream! As good as it was, what God was doing in our lives was vastly outweighing the things we once thought so important.

It wasn't long after we were out of school that God began to show us that his plans for us were way outside anything we could have imagined!

Our heart to help people discover what it meant to have a personal, intimate, eternal relationship with Jesus began to consume us. We were always looking for opportunities to share with others whenever the opportunity arose.

In the first months of 1980, I began to entertain the idea that my dream to be a businessman was going to be set aside for something God had ordained for our lives.

---

*I actually began to believe that God had
a call on my life.*

---

2 Timothy 1:9 (NKJV)

⁹ Who has saved us and called *us* with a holy calling, not according to our works, but according to His own purpose and grace which was given to us in Christ Jesus before time began,

Ministry

Sensing a call was the easy part. Sorting it out was another thing. At first, Anne was not on board. The idea of going back to school was hard to imagine. It's only been three years since I became the first Berry to ever graduate from college, and to think now that I might have to go back to school to prepare for ministry? No way! Giving up on my dreams, starting over was a mountain we on the outside didn't want to climb. But let me tell you what happened.

Over the next 21 months, Anne got on board and embraced our call. We also completed a ministry training program and pioneered our first church! All by the age of 26.

This was the beginning of the journey, and to make statements like we found ourselves Pastoring in all-white spaces in a small rural community with no people of color might seem odd, but it's part of the story of how God did such a fantastic thing.

At this time, I never thought about being white, being in all-white spaces, what that meant to me, and to others who weren't white. We had no idea that, at some point, very shortly, we would start thinking about it and how it was going to impact our ministry in the future.

We spent ten years in our first church, learning the basics of Pastoring and how to do that in a God-honoring way. We learned to exercise and develop spiritual muscles that would so be necessary for the next phase of our ministry.

Our love for the Word of God grew. We relished in the practicality of His word and how relevant it was to our everyday lives. Its impact on how we live and experience life. We also learned that it is not only important to love God, but that we also have a responsibility to love one another.

For ten years, we pastored a wonderful group of people in a small, all-white rural community who wanted to love God and learn how to live their lives for Him.

During this season, there would be times where I thought about the possibility of going to Des Moines and pioneering another church. At times when I would think about it, I would just put it down, because I worried that in my heart it was just because I wanted to do something in a bigger city. And things were going so well where we were.

Then something happened.

A friend of mine who had pastored in Iowa went to the mission field for a few years, contacted me and let me know that he was coming home and want to pray about starting a work in Des Moines. We offered to show him around and share what we knew about the city. I remember when he came, and I was driving him around thinking to myself, what are you doing? This opportunity should be yours; you are supposed to be the one coming here, but I just kept my mouth shut. He told me he was going to go home and pray about it. After a couple of weeks, he called me and said it wasn't right, and he wasn't coming.

In my heart, I heard the Lord say,

"If you don't go, I am going to send someone else."

Well, I wasn't having not of that. But, to leave, how do we do that? We were pastoring a great church; our kids were teenagers in a great youth group.

When we started our first church, we had nothing to lose. Now ten years later, to start over, what if it didn't work, our kids what about them. The idea seemed so risky.

Whenever you are venturing into the will of God for your life, you have to trust that He will provide everything you need to do what He is asking from you.

He told Joshua, "Be strong and courageous."

Joshua 1:6-7 (NLT)

6 "Be strong and courageous, for you are the one who will lead these people to possess all `the land I swore to their ancestors I would give them. 7 Be strong and very courageous. Be careful to obey all the instructions Moses gave you. Do not deviate from them, turning either to the right or to the left. Then you will be successful in everything you do.

Anne and I wanted to do this, but we worried about our children. In our hearts, we heard, "if you obey me, I will take care of your children." Another thing we thought about was, would we ever have people again who supported us as much as the ones in our present church?

Again, in our hearts, we heard, "If you obey and go, I will send you people to help, you won't be on your own." Would we have what it takes to build another work from scratch? This time God spoke through a friend. "Dan, God, has been preparing you for the last ten years for what He is about ready to do." When my friend said that I heard in my heart, "I have prepared you for the last ten years for what I am about ready to do."

Together, Anne and I decided that we had to go. We were in and would do whatever He wanted us to do. It's here that I began to wonder about the, "What I am about ready to do" part. I have prepared you for what I am about ready to do.

What did that mean?

2

A Call to Diversity...

As we were preparing to leave our first church, not only were we receiving confirmation and encouragement, something else was going on. Scripture says...

Proverbs 29:18 (NLT)

> [18] When people do not accept divine guidance, they run wild. But whoever obeys the law is joyful.

Other translations say, where there is no vision (redemptive revelations), the people will perish.

In this context, without guidance or vision, the new work would never get off the ground.

God began to speak to Anne and me about the new work he was calling us to and about our purpose there.

We knew how to start a "church" we had done that before, but in my heart, I began to wonder about what it would be like.

Would pastoring in a city be different from pastoring in a rural community? Would our vision change? Would our mandate be different?

Family ministry had become so important to us, helping families as they navigated their journey through life. We were young and raising a family ourselves, so it didn't seem that odd that our focus would be there.

In the middle of all the dreaming about this new work, I started hearing something I didn't expect. I heard a single word.

Diversity

Did I already mention that my world was white? Growing up in small rural communities in Iowa, my whole world was white. Our first church was in rural Iowa. It was 100% white. At the time, it was something that I never considered. Unfortunately, I'm not proud of this, but I could count my interaction with people of color on two fingers.

In the excitement of a new work and all that it was going to mean, something new began to happen in me. It started with that single word, diversity. What did that mean? I wasn't sure. I didn't even have a clue. I didn't share it with Anne for a while. If there is one thing I have learned about God, if it's something he wants to get across to you, it won't go away. Every time I would pray or dream about the new work, this word diversity kept coming up. It not only didn't go away; it began to consume my thoughts. I even started asking the Lord, what does this mean? He didn't say much, but what He did do was make it a desire in me, which led to it becoming a burden.

After a while, I did share it with Anne. We thought that maybe because we are going to a bigger city, it must mean that Black people would come to worship with us. We were naïve, uninformed, and ignorant about what God wanted to do. Could this be a big deal to God in a state that is 96% white, where most churches in the state are all white? In comparison, there were a few Black churches.

Obviously, it was important to Him. It was so important that the burden just kept growing larger. Before we even launched our first service, diversity had become an integral part of the heart of this new work.

Looking back, it all started with a word, that sprouted into a desire, that became a burden, that allowed something that seemed utterly impossible to happen. Isn't that the way God works? We only see from our perspective. We live out of our environments, but when God wants something, he has to interrupt the norm. He does that from the inside of us. In the beginning, it doesn't always make sense to us.

How cool is that? It made me wonder about how many things I might have missed out on because I didn't hear His still small voice, dismissed a word that he put in my heart, or because I didn't think it was relevant to us.

How many things have we labeled as being essential to God, but they weren't crucial? How many things were important to Him that we blew off because they weren't' to us?

We knew God was going to do a new thing, but in so many ways were clueless.

On July 7th, 1991, we had our first service. Our name was Cornerstone Family Church. I stood in front of a great group of people who were pioneers. I mention that because not everyone is willing to plow the ground necessary to start a new work. But there we were, worshiping, sharing God's word, and loving one another. I stood in front of that group of people and shared the vision God had given me. I opened up my heart and talked about where we were going to go, what our family was going to be like. We emphasized the importance of faith in the Word that God had given us and how we were going to change the world we lived in right here from Des Moines, Iowa. It's crazy, but all sixty of us really believed that!

I shared with them how we were going to help all people experience Christ in their lives, doing our best to teach them how to live for Jesus and realize their God-given purpose.

Without understanding the fullness of what I was talking about, I began to share that all people meant all people. God wanted to do a new thing and bring people from all walks of life together. As I stood before that lily-white congregation, I watched them embrace the idea of unity beyond a bunch of white people trying to get their act together. I had not yet realized it, but without diversity, there can be no unity. I was blessed to see it become a part of our conversations and blessed as it grew into being a part of our prayers.

In our all-white circles, we only understood divisiveness as the enemy trying to get us to fight with one another over how things should be run, over what kind of music we should have, what color the carpet should be. The only unity we understood was that we should all just get along with each other. The concept that the image of God wasn't genuinely represented by one ethnos wasn't even our radar; the idea that it took all ethnicities to reflect the true image, the fullness of God was not part of our thinking or beliefs.

I can hear people thinking, well there are no people of color in our communities, what are we supposed to do?

Not trying to presume I have all the answers to that, but a couple of thoughts are. It's not entirely true anymore. There are people of color showing up in every community, even in Iowa. Every year I participate in a bike ride across Iowa. It's called RAGBRAI. One year my youngest son, who happens to be African American, rode with me. We had stopped in a small town, probably no more than a thousand people. He leaned over and asked me, "Dad, do you think that there are any Black people in this town?" I said confidently, probably not Theo, and just as I said that a youngster who happened to be Black rode by us. He looked over at us and said, "Good Morning," and my son and I looked at each other and laughed, even in small-town, Iowa.

Another thing to consider is how we ended up so segregated, and why there are so few people of color living in our communities. There are reasons behind that. Maybe having a little historical understanding that there were constructs created in our past that made our communities what they are.

The good news is that if there were things in our history that shaped the demographic, then there can be things in our future that change that.

It's our prayer that the church leads the way.

Early on in this journey, the Holy Spirit took me to the gospel of John, where Jesus prayed his final recorded prayer before He was arrested and crucified. There is so much meaning in all of this, so much we should pay attention to. But something that the Holy Spirit genuinely caused to come alive in me was his prayer for oneness. That through that oneness, that perfect unity the world would be able to see Him, see the purpose of Him and understand how much He loves them.

John 17:1-21 (NLT)

[1] After saying all these things, Jesus looked up to heaven and said, "Father, the hour has come. Glorify your Son so he can give glory back to you. [2] For you have given him authority over everyone. He gives eternal life to each one you have given him. [3] And this is the way to have eternal life—to know you, the only true God, and Jesus Christ, the one you sent to earth. [4] I brought glory to you here on earth by completing the work you gave me to do. [5] Now, Father, bring me into the glory we shared before the world began.

[6] "I have revealed you to the ones you gave me from this world. They were always yours. You gave them to me, and they have kept your word. [7] Now they know that everything I have is a gift from you, [8] for I have passed on to them the message you gave me. They accepted it and know that I came from you, and they believe you sent me.

[9] "My prayer is not for the world, but for those you have given me, because they belong to you. [10] All, who are mine, belong to you, and you have given them to me, so they bring me glory. [11] Now I am departing from the world; they are staying in this world, but I am coming to you. Holy Father, you have given me your name;

now protect them by the power of your name so that they will be united just as we are. [12] During my time here, I protected them by the power of the name you gave me. I guarded them so that no one was lost, except the one headed for destruction, as the Scriptures foretold.

[13] "Now I am coming to you. I told them many things while I was with them in this world so they would be filled with my joy. [14] I have given them your word. And the world hates them because they do not belong to the world, just as I do not belong to the world. [15] I'm not asking you to take them out of the world, but to keep them safe from the evil one. [16] They do not belong to this world any more than I do. [17] Make them holy by your truth; teach them your word, which is truth. [18] Just as you sent me into the world, I am sending them into the world. [19] And I give myself as a holy sacrifice for them so they can be made holy by your truth.

[20] "I am praying not only for these disciples but also for all who will ever believe in me through their message. [21] I pray that they will all be one, just as you and I are one—as you are in me, Father, and I am in you. And may they be in us so that the world will believe you sent me.

The magnitude of this prayer cannot be overlooked. Why did He pray this? In his last prayer before leaving, it was all about the ones that were given him. That they would find their way into oneness, finding their way into realizing how important they all were to each other. How if they could pull this off, being one with one another, then the world would look their way and be open to the love that God has for them.

Could it be that He prayed this prayer because he knew that without it, it would be business as usual? That division and divisiveness would continue to run rampant in the human family? That we would continue to fight one another, climb over one another for positions of superiority? Remember, his disciples fought over who would be able to sit next to him in the afterlife.

Could it be that he knew that as soon as he left, Satan would infiltrate their ranks, segregate them by continuing to foster envy, jealousy, feelings of superiority among them? He didn't ignore this or pretend it wouldn't happen; He didn't stick His head in the sand. He prayed for us. He gave us His glory that we would be emboldened, empowered, to work against forces that would divide us and be one. He didn't pray that we would ignore it, stick our head in the sand, and deny its effect on our lives.

Segregation runs deep in the Body of Christ.

It runs across ethnicity, culture, denominations, and generational lines and a hundred other sub-categories.

On the surface, it may look as if this prayer has gone unanswered, but I have to believe that Jesus' prayer will come to pass, and don't you want to be a part of creating something that has always been in the heart of our Father.

This mandate of oneness is born out of His heart, so doesn't it make us all beholden to it? Do you remember what Paul said to the churches in Galatia?

Galatians 3: 26-29 NLT

> [26] For you are all children of God through faith in Christ Jesus. [27] And all who have been united with Christ in baptism have put on Christ, like putting on new clothes.
>
> [28] There is no longer Jew or Gentile, slave or free, male and female. For you are all one in Christ Jesus. [29] And now that you belong to Christ, you are the true children of Abraham. You are his heirs, and God's promise to Abraham belongs to you.

Paul is saying that the things, all the barriers, all the walls that we built, all the things we used to divide ourselves are gone, all the old barriers are done away with in Christ.

The churches at Galatia probably said, "Oh no, we just had a bunch of Jews here that told us if we really want to get close to God, we have to become like them, do things their way. And there are still men and women, and there are still slaves and free."

But what Paul is trying to get them to see is a new reality. In Christ, there are no barriers, no big I's and little U's…there's Jesus and the rest of us. Talk about a new reality! Please hear my heart.

We, as the Church, are commanded to usher in this new reality. As followers of Jesus, it is a big part of our responsibility to tear down these walls that divide us.

Ephesians 2:13-14 (NLT)

13 But now you have been united with Christ Jesus. Once you were far away from God, but now you have been brought near to him through the blood of Christ.

14 For Christ himself has brought peace to us. He united Jews and Gentiles into one people when, in his own body on the cross, he broke down the wall of hostility that separated us.

For you and me to follow Jesus means that it is our responsibility to eliminate these constructed barriers and embrace the unity Jesus prayed for. As a follower of Christ, we can't ignore these barriers we must work to remove them. That We Will All Be One.

The truth is that most of us had never thought about why there was so much segregation in the Body of Christ. The idea that God wanted us to be a part of the desegregation of the body was a new concept for all of us.

In the early days, all the talk about diversity, about bridging the divides, was easy to embrace. When you talk about something but aren't doing anything, it's not all that difficult. As time moved on, I have to admit I began to get a little discouraged because nothing was happening; no one from a different ethnicity was showing up. Another thing that happened was that some thought that I was talking too much about it. In my heart, I wondered if I had really heard from God, and if this vision was ever going to happen. My worries were not if we were going to survive as a new church; they centered around a "word" I believed God had given us. Was it ever going to come to pass?

And then it happened...

3

A Couple of Visitors...

During the first year of our ministry, unbeknownst to me, a friend of mine worked with an African American lady at a local publishing company. Her name was Elsie; she had a love for God's Word that was growing every day. She had become frustrated with the church and wanted more. In the breakroom, he began to tell her about our new work. "I have a friend who just started a new church a few months ago, just down the road from here. He loves the word of God like you, and he is a gifted teacher." (Thanks Mike) Mike told her she should go visit.

Sure, enough one Sunday morning Elsie, walked into our all-white space. I hope we didn't all stop and stare. It would have only been out of excitement. But I can't be sure. I can't imagine the courage it took for her to walk through those doors. She worshipped with us, she sat there and listened to the Word of God. "As long as the Word was being taught, I was going to be there," she would later tell us. She also remembered how my Dad had so warmly welcomed her with a big smile and hug.

Later she and her husband Burt became close friends with my parents.

Week after week, she kept coming back, participating in the service and serving wherever she was needed. She liked to tell me how she thought I was a great teacher. She would say to me that she was telling all her friends about me, and how she was going to a new church that was helping her in her spiritual walk. They would ask her about my name and the church location. She would tell them and invite them. Only later did she tell them that I was white and that the whole church except for her was white.

For the rest of that first year, Elsie would bring her family, some of her friends, and we enjoyed the beginnings of our diverse experience. I have to admit that, outside of being excited she was there, we gave little thought to how she was feeling. What was her experience and how was it affecting her life? She had left an all-Black church and was now attending an all-white church. We just kept doing what we were doing, the way we had always done church. We all loved Elsie, and she loved us. That was it. There was little or no desire to do things differently. We had an excellent opportunity to open our hearts to her and what she brought to the table. I wonder if she ever really felt part of our family. She came in, and we embraced her but never asked her about her needs or what we could do differently to make her feel more welcome in our all-white space. We never asked her about how she would do things. What were her thoughts and ideas were? We didn't give her a place at the table.

Anne and I took in foster children for years. Eventually, we ended up adopting five of them. We had three biologicals, and with the five adopted, we had quite a quiver of 8. As hard as you work to make everyone feel a part of the family, there are always issues. If you don't press and work hard to understand and be inclusive, it doesn't matter if they are stepchildren or adopted; in their minds, the stigma is always there. Beyond saying, 'I love you", you have to show interest, show openness; you have to let others in that will help you live outside of your bubble.

As much as we loved her, we never brought Elsie to the table. As I write this, my heart is sad. She opened the door, she came to help us do what God called us to do, but we never gave her a voice.

Paul dealt with this in his comparison of our physical bodies and the spiritual body.

1 Corinthians 12:18-27 (NLT)

[18] But our bodies have many parts, and God has put each part just where he wants it. [19] How strange a body would be if it had only one part! [20] Yes, there are many parts, but only one body. [21] The eye can never say to the hand, "I don't need you." The head can't say to the feet, "I don't need you."

[22] In fact, some parts of the body that seem weakest and least important are actually the most necessary. [23] And the parts we regard as less honorable are those we clothe with the greatest care. So, we carefully protect those parts that should not be seen, [24] while the more honorable parts do not require this special care. So, God has put the body together such that extra honor and care are given to those parts that have less dignity. [25] This makes for harmony

among the members, so that all the members care for each other. [26] If one part suffers, all the parts suffer with it, and if one part is honored, all the parts are glad.

[27] All of you together are Christ's body, and each of you is a part of it.

Why would we be so grateful that God had sent her to us, to help us realize this incredible vision of diversity and not give her a place at the table? Did we really think that we could make all the right decisions without her?

By the end of the year, we started picking up some momentum. Growing slowly but growing was good with us. At the end of the first year, we had an opportunity to move across the parking lot into a new facility that was way beyond our expectations. The new building held so much opportunity for growth, and that excited us. We all gathered our things and moved into a building that only God could have made possible. At that point, it was still just Elsie, but she was all in. To this day, I remain eternally grateful she didn't walk away. She may have been the only person of color attending, but the call to bridge, the mandate to bring people together was still burning bright in our hearts, and we weren't giving up!

During our first years, we had a radio program on a local Christian station. For 15 minutes every day, I would share the Word of God and how it could change your life if you learned how to apply it. I loved to teach the basics of God's promises and how they could help us in our everyday lives. That little program gave us a lot of exposure to our community and was a tool that brought many people through our doors.

Somewhere in the reaches of that radio signal, there was a young Black pastor who was picking up his wife from work. As he waited for her, it would just be the exact time our program was on. When she would get in the car, they would listen together. He would later tell her that they needed to visit this church. "It's right here in Des Moines, and this guy can really teach."

This young pastor's church was on the campus of Iowa State University in Ames, Iowa, about 35 miles north of the city. Whenever the school was on break, they wouldn't have services. One day, they showed up at Cornerstone. It just happened to be on a Sunday I wasn't there, but Pastor James and Tresa Ransom came and brought their family and worshiped with us. It must have been a pleasant experience because they came back. Anne and I had the opportunity to meet them. His personality, his gifting, his calling was all magnetic. It got to the place that whenever Iowa State was on break, the Ransoms came to worship with us. We enjoyed getting to know them. Before long, we were getting together sharing about ministry and being pastors. We spent so much time talking about the Word.

We got our churches together and began to share services. It was at BCC, Body of Christ Worship Center, that I got to experience the culture of the Black Church. Before long, it wasn't just Pastor James and his family. Whenever Iowa State was on break BCC, would not have services and would attend CFC with the Ransoms. Many from his own family began to trickle in and visit us because they trusted him, and they loved the Word. It would be an understatement to say that a door was beginning to open, but all of a sudden, our lily-white congregation was now starting to look more like what we imagined God wanted us to look like. Our dream was coming true. It was so cool to watch and to be a part of it. What was seemingly impossible, what many deemed as unnecessary and irrelevant, was beginning to manifest before our very eyes.

During the excitement and feelings of joy, Pastor James and I begin to have some serious talks about the possibility of the two of us working together. We talked about the possibility of our two callings being the same. That God in His master plan might have ordained that the two of us should labor together to bring about the answer to Jesus' prayer, to help build bridges across the divides that separated us ethnically and culturally.

Our all-white staff and leadership team decided that it was time for a change, and we offered Pastor James the position of Assistant Pastor. As we anxiously awaited his answer, none of us understood the magnitude of this offer and what it would mean for Him and his family. The opposition that he would face in coming to help us. Why would one of the Black communities up and coming brightest stars leave the community and go to work for a white church? My ignorance kept me from appreciating the magnitude of his decision. With all the history of misuse and abuse, lack of appreciation, superior attitudes, why would he take a chance? He could have said no, but he didn't. He actually accepted the position and became a part of the Cornerstone Family Church staff and family.

Body of Christ Worship Center had become a part of our family, like a sister church, and I don't want to leave their role in this decision out. Our gain was their sacrifice.

Here's something I have learned about God; our future is His past. As we move into our future, He's coming out of it. Part of trusting Him is knowing that He has already been where we are going. None of this was catching Him off guard or catching Him by surprise, provision for this change was in the works.

Our new season was upon us, but it wasn't just about us. A new season for Body of Christ Church in Ames was also on the horizon. God was preparing a young man by the name of

Minister Toran Smith and his wife Ana to fulfill their calling to take over the church and run with the vision God had placed in their hearts. We were all linked, had become family, and it was such a blessing for all of us to watch God work it all out.

Another aspect of this was that the vision for diversity was not just in our hearts now but in the heart of the new pastor who was taking over. I was a white pastor telling a predominantly white congregation that we were not going to remain a white church, that God wanted to bring His family together into oneness. It wasn't long before Pastor Toran was telling his predominantly Black congregation that they were not going to remain a Black church, that God wanted to bring His family together into oneness.

One ask, and a courageous decision on Pastor James' part, was now expanding this incredible vision from one house to two. Pastor James came in and was so respectful and submitted to his role. His heart was to be a blessing to me and to his new church family in whatever way he could. He loved people and didn't care what hue of brown you were. If he could get ahold of you, you were going to feel his love. He was large in every area of his life; a big man, a big heart for God and you, a big smile, and a big handshake and hug. He told me that a football coach had taught him when he shook someone's hand to look them in the eye and give them a squeeze that they wouldn't soon forget. The world, the stereotype, the narrative of racial difference wanted us to believe that someone like him was to be feared, but it all changed as I got to know one of the most loving men I have ever met.

I was not going to make the same mistake twice; he received a seat at our table, and can I say that it livened up our staff meetings. There were 6 of us at the table all white except for Pastor James, but he was ready. Our conversations around race, and what it meant to be a diverse church went to a whole new level. His boldness and lack of fear to broach subjects that made many of people uncomfortable were invaluable to us. Don't misunderstand me; he did it in a way that even though at times we were squirming, we wanted more, we couldn't get enough of it. His peaceful but uncompromising spirit captivated us. I loved to listen to Him, and we all learned so much from him. It's incredible how much we can learn from one another if we just make an effort to listen? In the beginning, we weren't as good at it as we should have been. We had moments of insecurity, moments where we didn't want to listen at all, moments where we got defensive, but His vulnerability and boldness garnered respect from all of us.

We listened and learned, and as we did, we opened our hearts to change. This lily-white staff and church were about to go through a transformation. Can you imagine what it must have been like for him to sit in an all-white space and challenge the status quo? To engage us in conversations that we, in the beginning, probably deemed unimportant. Unnecessary, why do we have to talk about this? Why is this important? As I look back on it all, the appreciation I felt for him at the time has now turned into respect. He didn't have to do what we now call the hard work of love, but he did. And it started our transformation into what we are now.

I feel like I need to share this now, even though we will get into this more later. But all of us at the table were immersed in our whiteness. Even though we were open and wanted to be a part of this vision, we were all clueless. The entirety of everyone at that table had never considered what it meant to be white. We didn't even think about what it meant to be white, or how it impacted other cultures, and specifically people of color. When Pastor James showed up and began to talk about race and the impact of racism, we all quickly became aware of our whiteness. Have you ever dreamed that you were up in front of a group of people without your clothes and had nowhere to run? That's how we felt.

Some walked away, but most hung in there. We began to deal with our whiteness by understanding that our way of experiencing life was not like everyone else. It was interesting how we all move along at different paces. Some didn't want to move at all. They stayed entrenched in their whiteness with little or no concern about where God wanted us to go. By the way, these are the ones who bolted. Others jumped in with both feet and couldn't get enough of it, and as it happened, they were the ones who got frustrated with others who were moving along in a way they thought was too slow.

We learned very quickly that not all white people and people of color would move along at the same pace. My wife and I were a classic example. We were not walking through this journey at the same speed. I used to get so frustrated with her because it seemed to take her long to get it. She was impatient with my pressuring. I think that if she heard, "Why don't you get this?" one more time she was going to bolt. There has to be grace given to everyone. It was hard for me to learn and embrace this, but every one that is moving, even if it is ever so slow, will eventually get there. By the way, I think she gets it more today than I do.

As fun as the staff meetings were, what I especially treasured was my one on one sessions with my new assistant pastor. Behind closed doors, the listening and learning went to a whole new level. Pastor James wanted this vision to work as much, if not more than I did. The reality is that there isn't a group of people that want this vision to work more than Black people. His heart to help me and help this family fulfill this vision was driving him. His heart to help me successfully pastor people of color was a huge topic in our one on one meetings.

I remember thinking, isn't Pastoring, Pastoring?

Although there are elements of pastoring humans that are the same, because humans come from different experiences and locations, it is going to be different. The idea that pastoring different people meant pastoring differently had escaped me. Our church was heavily involved in International Missions work, and I learned early on that to be effective in ministering to people from other countries and cultures, you needed to know something about where they come from. So many times, ministry leaders just want to minister the truth out of their understanding and experience with little thought of whom they are trying to minister to, and then wonder why they are not effective.

But the idea that this was true here, how did I miss that? Was I immersed and ministering in the belief that everyone in this country needed to measure up to where I came from? The idea that if I got it a certain way, you needed to get it that way also.

If men want to have a meaningful relationship with their wives, they better grow in their understanding of where they come from, what makes them tick, because even though they are human, the way they are going to relate is going to be different. Pastor James wanted me to understand that cultural differences were going to require the same grace and consideration. He let me graciously know that if I wanted to be successful in pastoring people of color, I had a lot to learn.

History gives context; context brings understanding;
understanding makes healing possible.

One of the first things he taught me was that Black people would love you, but don't mistake that for trust. That hit me. I got it. I understood it but never applied it to my relationship with people of color. Trust is earned. I knew that, but wow, it made me realize I wanted to earn trust from the people that I loved. How could that happen if I didn't understand where they were coming from, what they had been through, and were going through now? My perspective, my experience was not the same as others. Did I care enough to open my heart and listen? He wanted me to understand that people of color were coming and wanting to be a part of what we were doing. They had left all-Black spaces to come to this diverse experience but didn't want to be made to feel like stepchildren or foster kids who didn't really belong. Could it be that being a white pastor with a white staff and leadership, we could consciously or subconsciously portray the attitude that, "we are glad you are here, but in this house, this is how we do things? You just follow our rules and do things the way we do them, and everything will be just fine." These were just a couple of the many things we talked about, but oh did I realize that the education was just beginning.

4

Not What We Expected...

It wasn't long before the initial excitement of becoming a diverse church began to morph. So many unexpected things started to happen. In our determination to give our newest family members a voice and a genuine seat at the table, all of a sudden, we were confronted with something we had never given any thought or consideration, our whiteness.

I had never given any thought to whiteness being a culture. In my mind, I thought diversity was adding in other ethnicities and cultures to us. I am embarrassed to say I didn't realize that every other culture in the world had to measure themselves against the culture that I didn't even know existed. Did we really believe that when it came to human life and existence, we were the standard to which everybody needed to conform? Of course, we won't readily agree on this, but just give it some thought, and I will bet you can find some of those mindsets in your thoughts over the years.

This mindset, at some level, justified the colonization of the country we now live in. I am going to ask you to take a look at what is known as "The doctrine of Discovery." Fundamentally, the Doctrine of Discovery was the Catholic church in Europe saying to the Nations of Europe, whatever lands you find Christian leaders do not rule, those people are less than human. The lands are yours for the taking.

If you google it, there is a lot of information on it. I realize you may have never thought about it or even voiced this belief, but I am just asking you to give honest consideration to this thought or belief system.

It's human nature to resist when someone challenges your way of doing things. Do you remember when you entered your teenage years, and all of a sudden, the people (your parents) you idolized and worshiped began to morph into someone that you didn't think had a clue, how you thought your way was the best and how they just didn't understand?

It's the same culturally when you, as a white person, are confronted with the reality that there are other ways of doing things when people of color come to the table with a voice. There are these subtle biases that creep to the surface. All of a sudden, these things that make all white people uncomfortable, called supremacy, privilege, and fragility jump all over us and make us extraordinarily insecure. We become less open to some of the changes we need to make so our new family members can feel welcome.

In the infancy of our nation, Thomas Jefferson, who penned the words "all men are created equal" had to justify in his own heart his ownership of over six hundred human beings. Four hundred slaves were at Monticello and over two hundred at his other properties. In his book "Notes on the State of Virginia," he introduced the idea that people of color had to be inferior, somehow less than their white counterparts, a lower standard of species.

Therefore, people of color are not included in the "all men are created equal" belief. I also have to add that neither were women. It fostered a narrative that bled into our societal hierarchy that somehow, people of color were less than their white counterparts and introduced the belief in America that they were a substandard species. He challenged the world of science to prove this.

First of all, the narrative that race is biological, and one race is inferior to another has never been proven scientifically. In fact, it has been disproven. None the less, the toxic idea continued to grow as a fundamental belief within people who were white. The narrative led to the construct of race. It led to the misuse and abuse of people of color. It fostered a belief, whether embraced consciously or subconsciously, that white was better and supreme. Even when slavery was abolished, the narrative lived on. It justified our nation's leaders, who were all white men, to determine who could be a citizen of this country and who couldn't. It survived through years of Jim Crow laws, a system of state and local statutes that legalized racial segregation for a hundred-plus years. It supported twenty years of resistance to the civil rights movement and, to this day, contributes to our bias against people of color.

To ignore these biases, to pretend that we have not been affected, I have found to be both damaging and naïve. I have learned that most white people want to ignore our history, do not wish to be taught correctly about it, and do not want to take any responsibility for it. Yet, without history, there can be no context, and without context, there can be no understanding, and without understanding, there can be no healing. There can be no true racial reconciliation. How many times have we judged the actions or responses of Black people as being misguided or over the top because we did not understand the context? How could we ever understand if we continue to ignore history? If we continue to believe that all that stuff is over and doesn't deserve our attention.

Not long after Pastor James joined the pastoral team, we decided that he should be a part of the board of the church. As staff size increased, we were intentional about adding people of color. It looked to some that we were adding only people of color and that we were *only* considering people of color whenever a staff or leadership need came up. I could feel the nervousness of some as this intentionality began to manifest. Were the new leadership and staff appointments being considered *only* because they were Black? I can honestly say that was not the only thing we were looking at, but if we were serious about this vision, we needed to do this. We needed to diversify the table and those who had a voice and were making decisions about the direction of this incredible church God was putting together. When you have been "stacked" in one direction for so long, you have to take bold steps to change. God was so good to send us people who could help us facilitate this change.

Remember, in the beginning, the Lord told us that if we did what he asked us, he would send us people to help. At this time, he was sending us people of color to sit at the table with us.

For the most part, during this season, it was only nervousness that was manifesting among white members of the church. To the best of my ignorant self, I just tried to keep the focus on the mandate that God had given us. Doing that held us together and moving in the right direction.

I watched as we all began to do church together. As we started to build relationships, people took steps towards each other. White people were starting to recognize and embrace their interpersonal racism. Many would go to Pastor James and ask his forgiveness for their issues. Many Black family members were dealing with the cause and effect of racial trauma and trying to make it right with their white family members. It was during this time that we began to hear that it wasn't just white people who were racist, Black people were racist too. It wasn't only white people saying it; it was people of color chiming in on this line of thinking. The problem with this is that I don't think very many people understood the true definition of racism.

Definition of Racism

1. Racism involves one group having the power to carry out systemic discrimination through the major institutions of society. (government, courts of law, banks, schools) Institutions that create and support public policies
2. Social and institutional power plus racial prejudice
3. System of advantage and oppression based on race
4. A white supremacy system supported by an all-class collaboration called white, created to end cross-racial labor solidarity.[1]

People of color can be angry, prejudiced, and bigoted, but I don't think they have, as a collective group, engaged in and profited from Racism. Racism was constructed by people who held power and controlled the institutions that govern and control our lives. Some could argue that there are many Black coalitions and alliances, which is true, but even though they have accomplished great things, it has never been from a majority position that enabled them alone to change the system.

Whether it's government, courts of law, or our education systems, these systems were controlled by white men who used that power to subjugate people, affording advantage to some and holding back opportunities for others based on the color of their skin. That is racism, and that means the people of color can be many things, but racist is not one of them.

At this point, I realize that many will begin to feel extremely uncomfortable, but I ask you to continue for a little longer.

Don't give in to your temptation to put this book down.

It's normal to have these feelings; what's not normal is finding the courage to press forward. Can I graciously remind you that it is the truth that sets us free? There have been so many lies, and those lies have to be exposed so we can truly find our freedom and become the effective bridge-builders God wants us to be. There are a lot of things in the heart of Jesus that He wants us to be a part of, but this has to be foremost in His heart. Otherwise, why would he have prayed the prayer?

Earlier I had mentioned that when we started diversifying the leadership and staff tables, there was some nervousness beginning to manifest among some of the white ranks. This tension even occurred among staff. I could feel and see some of the staff members becoming a little weary of all the conversations around the subject of race. Ever heard, "Why does it always have to be about Race?" If truth be told, I know some were outright resistant and didn't want to be a part of it. There's a difference between being resistant because it's hard work and being against it altogether. So, even with all the sharing of vision and rejoicing over God bringing it about, there will always be those who don't get it and don't want to be a part of the process. White people do have the privilege not to participate if they don't want to, and it won't affect their lives, but people of color don't have that privilege, it's in their faces every day.

At some point in time, we had to realize that not everyone who starts with you will stay with you, let alone finish with you. It's true in any story, but when you add the racial element to it, it goes to a whole new level.

Did I mention a whole new level?

The Music

I have been pastoring a long time, pioneered two works, and if there is one thing I have learned, it's the style of worship that can be the most controversial thing in the church. Worship styles have split more churches caused more people to change churches, more than any other area. It is such an important element in most houses of worship.

Understanding the importance of music to Black people, one must grasp the historical beginnings of the Black church.

"Spirituals, field songs, and folktales made it possible for enslaved Africans to narrate their own experiences of oppression, God, community and life, and liberation on their terms. Black Worship's ability, over centuries, to affirm Blackness, empower Blackness, and acknowledge that Black bodies have something of worth to offer God and the world God loves."[2]

Although the Black church has provided an escape from the supremacy of white culture, the white church. It has allowed Black people to freely worship, to be themselves without the scrutiny of white people. Correct church history has proven out that the only reason the Black church exists is because of racism in the white church.

There are some white Christians who get very angry at that statement, but we cannot continue to deny or cover up the church's complicity in its support of chattel slavery.

I would like to recommend to those who are looking for more in-depth study into this, "The Color of Compromise" by Jamar Tisby.[3]

When we took our first steps to diversify our Worship is when we began to experience what I'll call backlash. When white people not only got nervous but manifested opposition to the necessary changes that were coming.

Our worship leader had been with us from almost the beginning, he was white and very well suited for a predominantly white church, which up until recently we had been. CCM, Contemporary Christian Music, fueled our expression. The only complaint we heard, in the beginning, was that we never did any Hymns.

The music, we understood, is a huge expression and would allow us to give our newest family members a real place at the table. It would allow them to express themselves as they would in the Black church, but also allow white members to learn and experience new elements of worship. Most Black people are very accustomed to the white worship style, but I don't think you can say that about white people.

I have not met many people who didn't love it when a Black choir performed. The energy and passion that Black gospel exudes is such a blessing. But when you intend to bring it to your table regularly, it interrupts whatever it is that you have created out of your own wants and likes, what you have deemed as the best way to worship God. Every culture has its expression, preference when it comes to music, but are we open to learning to worship with a multicultural expression?

At this stage of the church, we had become quite diverse but were still doing a white expression of worship primarily. We had to open the door for our Black family members.

Pastor James' wife Tresa was extremely talented in the area of music, so we approached her with the idea that she could help us develop a choir and begin the process of helping us experience a new expression of worship. In place was a highly effective worship team that had helped us worship every week for the past couple of years. I thought this was going to be an exciting time as we navigated this. I thought it was going to add to an already fantastic experience. I've previously mentioned how naive' I was, and wow did it manifest in this area.

Our worship leader continued to lead, and Tresa came alongside to help in the development of our new expression. In no time, we had a fully functioning choir, as many people of color quickly jumped on the bandwagon to be a part. We started off doing our regular worship with our predominantly white team, followed by a predominantly Black choir. It quickly became very apparent that there were basically two teams doing their own things. In the beginning, it seemed ok, but the element of personal preference began to show up. Tresa wanted to be a part of this journey even though she knew the opposition that would be right around the corner. She purposefully held back and tried to give space for adjustment and acceptance. Can you imagine how that felt, to have to compromise who you are and the gifts you have so that they can be accepted and appreciated in a predominantly white space? While most of us who were white were worrying about our preference and what made us feel most worshipful, our family members of color were worried about being accepted and appreciated. Was there going to be unified progress, or would it only end up being a mess and cause a boatload of rejection?

Our worship leader at the time was not a real part of bringing this vision about. In staff meetings, he seemed somewhat agreeable, but, in all actuality, was not on board for what needed to happen. Some felt that he was only doing what He thought he was being made to do, but only barely. I have always said that some of the most insecure people in the world are people in the ministry. Insecurity, fear of others, fosters nothing but bad stuff. How can you open your heart to a new way of doing things if you are not secure in who you are? You must understand that your job as a minister is to bring people along in the development of their gifts. When you tolerate or oppose someone else because they are different from you, it's ungodly. We heard, "I have never done it that way before" and "I can't do that or do it that way" a lot. What we didn't hear a lot was, "I have never done it that way, but I'm willing to learn." In the midst of this season, some faithful people wanted to help and opened their hearts to be a part of the incredible change.

As things began to develop, it became evident that we needed a new leader in the music department. It was during a summer camp meeting that I made the decision to make a change, and I dismissed the leader. This decision was huge, because we loved this guy and what he brought to the table in the early years of our ministry, but it was his time to go. Remember, not everyone who starts with you will finish with you. Watching what was going on for almost two years made the decision easier for me. What I didn't expect was the reaction from the church family.

It was here that we experienced our first "White Flight." It was here that internal nervousness turned into outright opposition. It was here that some set aside the vision and made a decision to leave out of pure preference. We lost people who pioneered with us who had been hearing about the vision from the very beginning. We lost some friends over this decision. Only a few expressed their displeasure over the decision. Most just left without a word. I remember that one Sunday morning, there was a letter on the windshield of my car, blasting my decision and stating they weren't coming back. I'd be lying if I didn't tell you that both Anne and I were surprised and hurt or that during these times, we weren't nervous. In this first exodus, I never knew the terminology or the definitions of White Privilege or White Fragility. Therefore, I didn't have a clue as to what was going on in their hearts that they would vacate like that. I just assumed that they were too big of fans of the previous worship leader to embrace the vision God had given us. Maybe they were too much into themselves and what they wanted instead of what God wanted. If I were ever going to be able to survive my assignment, it would be essential to learn about these things, White Supremacy, White Privilege, and this thing called White Fragility.

Our quest for a new worship leader began. In the beginning, I was determined to look outside for someone who could come and do both white worship and Black worship, someone who got it and could do it. I'm not saying there wasn't someone out there that could do it, but we never found them. By this time, we had transitioned from Tresa leading the choir, to her sister Tina taking over. At first, I was so determined to find someone from the outside to bring a fresh start that I wasn't even considering anyone in the house. I even asked Rev. Tina, who at the time was now leading the Worship, to help me in the search. Later I learned that she was disappointed not to have been considered. Can you imagine having a gift and wanting to share it and not even being considered. Then, on top of that, being asked to find someone from the outside to do what is in your heart to do?

I had just experienced my first white flight and was so nervous about making the right decision. In my mind, it had to be someone who could make both groups of people happy. The idea of coming up with our own voice, our own sound, was completely escaping me.

Anne and I were having lots of conversations about this. I remember that during one of them, she told me the Lord had spoken to her. She said that He had told her that the person we were looking for was already with us. I asked her if He said who? She said yes, it was Rev. Tina Williams, our Worship leader. When she told her name, I knew it was God.

I would understand if she felt like she was our second choice, but she wasn't. When she became our Minister of Music, I'm sure it wasn't easy. Tasked with the job of making our worship something that could be enjoyed across cultural lines was not going to be an easy task. In the beginning, I expected that she would solely be the one to do it. Whenever she would let others on the worship team lead, I would oppose it. I wanted one worship leader, but we found out that blending music was not easy. The problem is authenticity. To have it, you have to have authentic people in specific genres of music. Tina could sing CCM music, but Tina had to be Tina. I was so afraid to have a Black person sing Black music and a white person sing white music because I was worried, we'd end right back where we were, with two competing groups. I put a lot of pressure on here to find a way to do it herself.

It is here I learned that not all the pressure she was feeling was from white people and their fear of losing white music. A lot of pressure was coming from me. My fear of losing more white people was manifesting more than my faith in what God had called us to do. There was no question that we were honoring her and giving her a place at the table. But my micromanagement and demanding something of her she couldn't deliver caused her a lot of frustration and disappointment. No doubt, she was wondering if she had made the right decision. But here's the thing, she didn't quit. We didn't give up and walk away. We did the best we could to trust God and let Him guide us through this transition.

How did we become authentic?

One of the first things we did was combine the worship team and band with the Choir. No longer two teams, but one. Another thing that had to happen was that we allowed other people to share their gifts. For a season, we continued to lose some white families. It was hard for all of us, but especially for Tina, because it showed that people still had a problem. No one would ever say the real reason why they were leaving. They would come up with any reason they could find other than the truth, but we knew.

You might ask how we survived all of this? That's a question we have asked ourselves multiple times, and the only answer we can come up with is we didn't give up. We asked for a commitment to the cause. I remember one Sunday morning; the Lord instructed me to bring Tina before the congregation and recognize the challenges that she was facing and pray for her. The Holy Spirit fell on the place, on her, and the congregation. It was an incredible moment that brought her love and support from the rest of us. I'm not saying that all the difficulties were over, but from that point on there was no looking back. We were in and committed to making it work.

I recently read in "United by Faith," about the 75% rule. If you are going to be in a multicultural church, you have to live by this rule. Not everything, not 100% of what goes on in the music of the church, can be what you require. Be happy with

75% and give the other 25% to your brothers and sisters of another culture and be satisfied with it. In reality, if you live according to this rule, everyone is going to get 75%. We have more in common than we realize, but that 25% messes with us.[4]

People choose many reasons why they attend a certain church, but the vision is not high on their lists. So, if you are a vision run church, that can be a problem. We just kept preaching: love God, love the people, love the vision.

When you discover that God calls people not just pastors to be a part of specific bodies to help carry out the vision, it changes why you go to church.

As many were walking away, God was sending in the new. Even though there were times that we didn't know if we were going to survive, we didn't let go of the plow. Nor did we let go of one another. We kept coming back to that prayer Jesus prayed. We wanted to be a part of the answer, and I guess we were naïve enough to believe this time it was going to come to pass. To this day, we still struggle to maintain our new voice and walk this vision out. But there's no going back.

I can remember when we finally settled in and felt good about what was going on musically. I felt like we were beginning to find our voice, our sound. In life, we know that the end of a battle does not mean the end of the war. In life, there are always new battles to be waged. It's easy to forget that sometimes.

Pastor James was doing everything he could to help me and educate me to pastor a diverse family successfully. Continuing education was a big part of our ministry, so much so that every year we all attended some sort of leadership seminar. One year he asked about attending a leadership seminar in Temple Hills, MD. He told me that Pastor John Cherry was someone he had great respect for and had been mentored by him for several years. Plans were set in motion for him to go. I decided at the last minute to go with him — thinking that it would be an excellent opportunity for us to spend some time together and get to know each other a little better, which turned out to be a divine act of fate.

We arrived at the Dulles International airport in Washington, DC, and I have to admit that I had not even looked into what we were attending. He made all the arrangements, and I was just along for the ride. When we arrived at the airport, the hosts of the leadership seminar were there to greet us and get us to our hotel. From that moment until we departed, I have never experienced such warmth and excellence in my life. This event was a leadership conference for pastors hosted by Pastor John Cherry and his church, an African Methodist Episcopal Church, known as From the Heart, in Temple Hills, Maryland (a suburb of Washington DC). When we finally arrived at the opening service, I found myself in a mostly Black space. There were several thousand people there to celebrate the Lord and the opening of the leadership conference. It was here that I was exposed to the ministry of Pastor John and Rev. Diana Cherry for the first time. They pastored a church of 26,000 plus members. At this point, I thought I had never heard of them. Mrs. Cherry opened the service, and Pastor Cherry gave the opening message; I was mesmerized. Their hearts for people, for pastors, gripped mine. It's funny how you can meet someone for the first time, sitting in a crowd of thousands and make a connection that would become life changing.

The next day Pastor James and I made our way to the opening day of the conference. Having attended several of these types of events over the years, my expectations were not all that high. When we entered and got settled, I noticed that this was literally an all-Black space. As I looked around, there were no white people other than me at this conference. For the first time in my life, I was the minority. As Pastor Cherry began to share from his heart about the week ahead, all my surroundings faded away. When he started to teach, I began to learn. As his heart for leaders was exposed, mine was drawn to his. After that opening session, I was overwhelmed. I think Pastor James thought I was overwhelmed because of the space I was in, and he kept asking me if I was ok. But the reality was Pastor Cherry's heart, and teaching had so connected with me. As I listened to him, I realized that there were no people of color speaking into my life other than Pastor James. White leaders and authors had mentored me all my spiritual life. I was attempting to pastor a diverse space, and I hadn't even given that a thought. As I sat at that conference, I realized that things needed to change. Being the only white pastor there at the time, I stood out. One thing I am grateful for is that it did not escape Pastor Cherry's attention, and it allowed me to meet him personally.

Little did I know that God had ordained me being there and that this man was going to impact my life more than anyone I had ever met.

The next year Pastor James and I, along with our wives, returned to the Conference. That year Pastor and Mrs. Cherry visited Cornerstone in Des Moines. I was so excited for him to see and experience what God was doing at CFC. Our relationship was growing, and our connection was deepening-the third year, we took the Board of the Church with us to the Leadership Summit. We were excited for them to see and experience what we had been talking about for the last two years. In the midst of the Summit that year, the Lord spoke to Anne and me that the Cherry's were to become our Pastors.

We had talked to the board about it after the evening session, and everyone was thrilled. The board could see and sense the Lord's leading in this. The next morning after the session, Anne and I approached Cherry's and somehow got to them both. I was so nervous, but we were able to share with them what the Lord had laid on our hearts and asked them to consider being our pastors, our Spiritual leaders. I will never forget their response; it was such a blessing to have them gather us into their arms as they began to pray over us and accept us and their new role in our lives. I don't think that we got too much out of the rest of the meetings because of what had just happened. For the first time in my life, since I had gone into ministry, I felt like I had a Pastor. God was so in it, and we were overwhelmed with excitement. We were no longer living and breathing all-white spaces. Our world had changed, not because of any other reason than we followed the dream God had put in our hearts.

I entitled this chapter "Not What We Expected" and does that describe what happened next.

We went home and could hardly wait until we could share it with our church family. By this time, Pastor and Mrs. Cherry had been to CFC, and we had all had the opportunity to experience them and get to know them a little better. His heart and his ability to teach the word in my heart were unmatched. He was not afraid to expose the ills of religiosity and teach God's Word in a manner that so many could grasp it.

Sunday morning came, and I was so excited to share what had happened, most responded with excitement and happiness for Pastor Anne and me. I spent some time reliving our journey into this place and sharing what had happened. How I believed that God had led us into a deeper connection with the Cherry's and the ministerial organization they had formed for ministers like us. Granted, I was going to step away from the organization that I had been a part of from the beginning of my ministry, but I felt this was God's leading to help grow me to effectively pastor this diverse family that God had entrusted to us. For us to keep going, this was something that needed to happen.

I remember going to lunch that day with such excitement in my heart about our future. The next morning, the rumblings started — emails, phone calls that, in the beginning, were just people sharing their nervousness about our next steps. People were asking me if we were going to become Methodist? What kind of role would Pastor Cherry have in our church, would my message change, my beliefs change, to name a few? I decided to have a town hall meeting of sorts and allow people to ask their questions. It sounds like a good idea, right? After what happened, some might think that I regretted doing it, but it had to happen. It exposed who was with us and who wasn't. Some of the questions were fair, but many were asked to trap me, and put a negative light on what was going on.

When that meeting ended, I was discouraged and afraid. Some were misunderstanding and misconstruing what God was doing — making this out to be a bad thing and not what God was intending. Once again, white families started to bail. While it wasn't that many, the way some of them left was hurtful. Reasons varied, but I do believe that race played a big part. The enemy began to attack my mind. I was losing sleep, and every time I prayed, it felt like God was ignoring me. On Sunday's I'd preach my heart out, kept doing what I had always done, and on the surface, all was good. But I was worried that I had turned the ship too fast. Was this it. Was it over before it started? After a few weeks of second-guessing myself, I started listening to my heart and got a grip.

I know this isn't super encouraging, but during this time, I was wondering if God was ignoring my valent efforts to keep this thing going. One morning I woke up, and I could have sworn that God was sitting next to my bed, and I heard him say,

"I just wanted to see how serious you were about what I have asked you to do."

If we are going to be a part of bridging the divides in the Body of Christ, you need to understand that it is going to cost you something. You will have to die to yourself and do the hard work of love. Isn't that what Jesus has asked us to do anyway? The reward will be incredible.

I know I heard the voice of God, and when I heard that, there was no turning back. It was "game-on."

Word was starting to get around the community about what God was doing in our midst. More and more Black people were starting to come into our family. I was beginning to gain some confidence and started enjoying this new family that was coming together. One morning I received a call from one of the ministers who was a part of the local Black Ministerial Alliance. He mentioned that he would like me to come to their next meeting. I readily agreed. In my naivety, I thought they were going to celebrate with me in how God was bringing people together across ethnic and cultural lines. Before the day came, one of my new Black minister friends got wind of what was going on and told me he wanted to go with me.

He never told me why he wanted to go, and I didn't ask. The day came, we went and walked into the meeting. There were about ten pastors there sitting in a circle. As soon as we sat down, it turned unpleasant. There was no celebration of the great work we were doing. They informed me that the Black Community was off-limits, and they didn't need my help to minister to their people. The wanted me to know that CFC had devastated one of the Black churches by taking a good number of its members, and we needed to stop trying to get more Black people to come. I was shocked, dumbfounded, but decided to listen and hear them. Almost everyone at the table had something to say, and I just sat there and listened. Some honestly appreciated what was happening, but felt like it was going too far. They wanted me to stay out of their community. My friend listened with me and tried to put a positive light on what we were doing and assured them that I was not recruiting their members, but other than being a comfort to me, he wasn't changing any minds. It was here that I learned something about church history in Des Moines.

Remember, history gives context, and context brings understanding. One of the pastors there who was a well-known businessman in the community spoke up and gave me the history. He told about a Baptist church here in Des Moines that was predominantly white and how there was a time where there seemed to be some healing happening across the ethnic divide. Many Black people started attending the church, and it became a pretty diverse community. What was happening at CFC had happened there 35 years before. Everything was fine until the young people who didn't have the problem their parents had, started doing life together. Some even wanted to date across these sacred divides, and it caused an issue.

Church leaders got together and decided that the Lord was leading them to start an inner-city work. There is nothing wrong with that, but their motive was to ask all the Black people to leave and attend this new work. Money was put behind it, and all of the Black families were conveniently asked to leave and help get it going. A lot of the pastors sitting around that circle that day were around when this happened — experienced all the pain of how and why that was done. After he finished the story, he asked me, or told me (I don't remember), that he knew I was going to do the same and they weren't going to let it happen.

I made a statement that the only reason we have a Black Church and a White church is because of racism in the white church. It makes some of my white brothers and sisters mad, especially in the evangelical church, but the reality of what happened here in Des Moines has been a part of the Church in this country from the beginning.

So many other events over the years came to challenge and discourage us. It seemed we were getting caught off guard every time we turned around. It would have been easy to quit, but on the flip side of all this, there was a lot of good going on. People were experiencing the richness of our diversity. The new relationships that were being born across these divides were one of the most rewarding things I have ever experienced. So many of us were just having fun and thrilled to be a part of what was going on. So, even with some of the behind the scenes stuff that was challenging, what was going on in our services in the church was thrilling and enriching.

5

Together but Separate...

During the early years, there was a lot of talk about reconciliation. It's such a biblical term. We mostly understand that what the Father God did in Jesus restored us, reconciled us into a perfect relationship with Him. Once lost, now found, once blind, but now we see.

We also understand that the restoration, the reconciliation was not just vertical, but also afforded us as God's kids the opportunity to be reconciled with one another. Reconciliation can mean to restore relationships. It can mean coming into agreement, living harmoniously.

It was a joy watching people who were a different ethnicity; people who came from a different culture move towards each other. As relationships were being built, interpersonal elements of racism were coming to the surface, and some people were making confessions. People were embracing their biases. Some denied that racism was affecting them in any way, shape, or form. "I'm not racist." "I'm color blind." "I have a Black friend." These statements were common and floating around.

We were so excited at the beginning of this. We didn't even realize more depth of communication was necessary if there was going to be real bridge building. When you see the church growing, people from all walks of life coming together to worship and serve Jesus, you don't want to go deep, but the question that had to be dealt with is: would it last?

Just because you have a diverse space does not mean that there is going to be any repair. Being civil to each other is good, but how does that relate to the dismantling of the structures that divide us.

Theologian Justo Gonzalez writes, "The multicultural vision is sweet. But there is a bitter side to it. There is the bitter side of having to declare that the vision of many peoples, many tribes, many nations, and many languages involve much more than bringing a bit of color and folklore into our traditional worship services."[5]

Let's help people experience Jesus, and everything will be fine. Then we won't have to talk about the issues that affect our lives. That has created the chasms that divide us. We won't have to do any bridge-building; or anti-racism work, we can just talk about it and feel good about our diverse family.

When young, I learned that if you made the right decisions, and worked hard that you would do fine, be able to realize the American dream. The reciprocal of that is if you make bad decisions and don't work hard, you won't do well -end of the story. Well, if that were the end of the story, that would be good, but it's not. When I saw anyone, a white person, or a person of color that wasn't doing well, I surmised in my mind, bad decisions, and not willing to work hard. What no one ever told me was that throughout history that there were systems put in place that put people of color at a disadvantage based strictly on their skin color, which had nothing to do with the decisions they made or how hard they worked. That there was this thing called privilege. Things that were built into our government, our laws, our schools, banks, and real estate opportunities that gave white people a leg up all the while holding people of color at bay by not making the same opportunities available to them. Even to this day, the average net worth of white families is 8 to 10 times greater than the average Black family.

How can I say I love you with the love of the Lord and ignore these issues that still impact your life? How can I stick my head in the sand and pretend like they don't exist, get mad when anyone brings it up, and say I love you? How can I get angry at others who are trying to help people of color by actively exposing all the injustice and say I love you with the love of the Lord? There has to be more to this. The reality is that love demands action.

In the beginning, the thing that concerned me most was that we were so politically divided. I thought it might interrupt the Kumbaya thing we had going on. Anti-racism work wasn't even on my radar. Most white evangelicals are very conservative politically. God, family and country and don't mess with that. The Republicans' platform in their minds was the closest to what they believed was biblically based; therefore, it created a huge voting block that most republican candidates catered to strategically and precisely. They did it so well that somewhere along the line, this Nationalistic mindset became more important to most than the teachings of Jesus.

Blacks, on the other hand, were mostly Democratic in their voting. In the beginning, I was a little confused about this. Okay, a lot confused. I understood that most Blacks in our church were very conservative biblically, yet liberal when it came to choosing their political candidates. I have to admit it was hard for me to even engage in conversations across the aisle, so to speak, because I had drunk the Kool-Aid and took the posture that if Jesus were here, he would surely be a Republican. I didn't get how you could be a Christian and embrace some of the things Democrats believed. I never said it, but I sure thought it. So, I just avoided having those conversations, even though I was encouraging others to have them.

Instead of loving and trying to understand my diverse family, I took the cowardly, hypocritical stance and avoided the conversations altogether. My approach to this was that even though we were voting differently, let's make sure that we don't fall apart over this. Let's take advantage of the opportunities we have to sit at the table with people who had different political views and learn from each other. Well, as you can imagine, that didn't go so well. It didn't go at all. I'm sorry to say that I was even espousing something that I was not doing. It was too much to engage, and most didn't want to risk what was happening, so we, for the most part, just avoided talking at all. I just settled into encouraging people to register, vote, and participate in the process. I have to note here this was all before Facebook and Donald Trump, so it worked well.

A church family can really avoid getting personal. You bump into people, throw out a few Praise the Lords, and off you go. Even where friendships were developing, there wasn't much depth in relationships manifesting. Nothing was happening to shake up our status quo, so we just kept doing the reconciliation thing and became very comfortable with our lack of depth. As I look back on it,

We were in a marriage with no intimacy.
How long could that last?

It was during this time that we were gaining a lot of respect. Word was getting out about us. People were amazed that God was doing this in a place like Iowa. Pastor Cherry would shake his head sometimes and express that it was hard for him to grasp that God was doing this in Iowa. Even in the white community who didn't understand what all that was involved, we were catching their attention. Who wouldn't be excited about people coming together from different ethnicities and cultures, especially if it wasn't affecting them directly?

One time we wanted to initiate a new program at the church that would help us do a little more life together. We paid to have a consultant come in and help us get this new initiative off the ground. He was somewhat familiar with our ministry and had expressed respect over the years for what we were doing as it related to cross-cultural ministry. He came and helped us develop a strategy for the new initiative, and while he was here, he threw in an overview of how he thought the church was doing as a whole. He interviewed staff, visited services, the whole nine yards. When he presented the report, he recognized some critical gaps and encouraged us to make some changes, and if we did, he was sure we would continue to grow to the next level. Before he finished, I could tell he had something else to share with me. He began to express how he felt the whole emphasis on the Black-White thing was hindering us. That we should back off of it and focus on the other elements of our calling. If anyone is reading this book and thinking that any aspect of this calling is going to be easy, think again.

From Cain and Abel, the devil has used our differences to divide and conquer us. He is good at wearing us down, discouraging us, making us second guess ourselves, lose our confidence. When the Lord spoke to me and wanted to see how serious I was about what he had asked me to do, He knew what was coming at us. He knew we would have a million opportunities to quit and walk away. The man sitting across from me had no idea what was going on in my mind. I was thinking here we go again. I couldn't believe he would even bring this up.

I suppose in his mind; his job was to help me grow the church; he was a consultant. But at this point, it was not some pipe dream we had. It wasn't some cool thing we were trying to do. This was a mandate, a calling. We really did believe that we were supposed to be a part of the answer that Jesus had prayed for. It had become a mandate that we could not walk away from.

Why are we doing this, taking this on? Especially when others decided they didn't want to be a part and walked away. So much of what had happened in our church up to this point aligned with what naysayers were bellowing, but now it was making me a little angry.

In our hearts, we wanted to do this right, be successful, and build these bridges, but we didn't want to destroy anything in the process. We weren't trying to chase people away, but the call was the call. As people questioned what we were doing and why we were making the decisions we were making, we would always take them back to Jesus' prayer. God asked us from the very beginning to be a part of healing the racial divide that has plagued the body of Christ.

African Americans have to deal with the effects and impact of interpersonal and systemic racism every day of their lives. Even though it's supposed to be different in the church, for the most part, it has not been. People of Color are told they are loved, but it seems that whenever an issue comes up, or an opportunity to help avails itself, most of us who are white want to stick our heads in the sand and ignore it. We espouse the truth, but when it comes to the truth as it relates to our history around race and our complicity in the constructions of race, we don't want to face it.

Another thing we can do is walk away. We can choose not to engage, we can go to an all-white space where we don't have to deal with these things, things that make us uncomfortable. It really is a privilege we have. Because we are the majority, we can choose to disengage, and throughout our history, it is what we've usually done.

I said all that to say this. In my heart and I believe in the hearts of a majority of our church family, we had decided that this is the mountain we will die on. If this ship is going to sink, it will sink not because we quit, but because we were doing exactly what the Lord had called us to do.

"I just wanted to see how serious you were about what I had asked you to do."

A lot of the opposition we were getting up to this point had very little to do with any type of anti-racism commitment. I don't think that most of us even knew that was part of it. All of the resistance was coming to us during what I call our "Kumbaya" stage. For twenty plus years, we just did the reconciliation thing, told each other how much we loved each other, and avoided any issues that would compromise that. It was like we would come together in our services and avoid talking about anything personal in our lives that we needed help with.

It was like if someone with cancer walked up to me and I knew they had cancer, but if I didn't talk about it, ask them any questions about it, I wouldn't have to make their issue my issue. I love you, but your issue is too big for me, and I don't have time or the energy to get involved, so let's just smile at each other and be on our way. It will be too much work for me to get involved and try and understand what you are going through. We weren't that cold-hearted, but going deeper was not something we were intentionally going after.

6

See No Evil...

We have thrown the word diversity around a lot. I have shared how we are the most diverse church in Iowa. People ask me how I know that, and I just said we were, with nothing really to back it up. It could have been an ego thing, but it seemed it was born out of the reality that we were proud of the fact that we had people from almost every culture and ethnicity worshiping with us. Whenever I described Cornerstone, you can bet the word diversity was going to be one of the adjectives used to describe who we were. It very quickly became what we were known for.

At some point, I was made aware there was some resistance to the word diversity. Not necessarily the word itself, but what it represented. To some white people, it somehow made them feel that there was something wrong with all-white spaces. To some people of color, it bothered them because it seemed if you could latch onto the word, then you were doing all the work that needed to be done, at least when it came to anti-racism work. That was us. For twenty plus years, we focused on reconciliation without really doing the hard work of love. Without even trying to understand the repair that needed to be done. Without giving any consideration to the effect that racism had and still has on our brothers and sisters of color. We were so bent on moving forward that we didn't realize we needed to embrace the past and find context. Without finding context, we were stuck.

We thought our most significant work was to be intentional about making sure our diverse family was not retreating into circles of fellowship that did not reflect our desires. How do we get the Black, brown, and white groups to mix? Build relationships with each other? It seemed like every time there were gatherings, people would retreat into groups that were homogeneous in nature. It was almost like I had forgotten Pastor James' words to me about digging deeper into the Black American experience and what my Black family members were still dealing with every day of their lives. We had become pretty proud of the fact that we had a diverse leadership team, diverse staff, and how we had diversity in every team in the church.

So, when it would start to look less diverse, we would jump all over that and work to maintain the appearance of a diverse team. I wonder now how much of that was just for the show. It sure wasn't building any bridges, fostering any depth in relationships, wasn't causing any kind of a cultural shift to manifest. We were worshiping together, and people were nice to each other, kind to each other. We were being Christ-like to each other, or were we?

At our twenty-year mark, we had a little celebration. It was twenty years at Cornerstone, and Anne and I's thirtieth anniversary in ministry. It was fun to celebrate. Our church family came together and celebrated us as their pastors, and we celebrated what God had done in our midst over the last twenty years. So many had experienced a personal encounter with Jesus. Our church was making a difference in people's lives. There was a lot to be grateful for, and we were, but it was about this time that I began to feel like something was missing.

Had we become too comfortable in our approach to fulfill the vision God had given us?

Were we talking a lot about bridging ethnic, cultural, denominational and generational lines, but not really doing it?

I could not shake the feeling that even though things on the surface were so good, something was not right. Have you ever gone through a season in your life when you felt like everything was going the way it was supposed to, yet in your heart, you knew something was missing? That maybe a change was coming. Well, that's precisely how I began to feel.

At this point, my prayers that I approached God with were all questions. Lord, what are we missing? What do we need to do? What changes do we need to make? As it related to our vision, I told the Lord that I was confused, needed His direction, needed His wisdom, admitted I wasn't sure where we were missing it. I asked for Help!

Sometimes for God to take you somewhere, He has to show you where you are. It makes sense because when you use a map or google maps to get directions anywhere, you have to put in your present location. I don't care where you want to go on this planet, you can get there, but only if you know where you are.

Psalm 119: 105 Amplified

105 Your Word is a lamp to my feet and a light to
my path

Sometimes we don't really know where we are, and that can be embarrassing. Your pride can get in the way when you think you are one place and find out you're in another. That's what happened to us. We thought we were so progressive and that we had built some great bridges. We thought we were in one place but found out we were in another.

Here's what happened. As I was asking all my questions to God, feeling like we were missing something, talking about how confused I was, and really needed His help, He showed us where we were.

On February 26, 2012, Trayvon Martin, an unarmed 17-year-old young Black man, was killed by George Zimmerman, sparking a national controversy. This event blew up in the news and was in your face whether you wanted it to be or not. People across ethnic lines began weighing in, and you could feel a polarization starting to ignite in our country over this event.

Do you remember that incredibly diverse family I was gloating over a few pages ago? We quietly avoided talking about what was going on. Even within our staff and leadership, we found ourselves just about voiceless.

I don't blame anyone for this but myself, but all of a sudden, I realized I had no voice. I did, but I did not know what to say to my diverse family. I offered nothing because I was afraid that I was going to offend someone. I believed that if I said something wrong, it would make things worse. As events around this shooting began to unfold, I am embarrassed to say that I just wished it would be over and we could move on. My whiteness and my privilege started crawling out all over me.

My thoughts went to defending why something like this could and would happen. I assumed this young man did something he wasn't supposed to. If he would have just done what I would have done, he would somehow still be alive. It was like my mind would not let me even consider that George Zimmerman could have been at fault. Even the media took the approach of trying to find something wrong in this young man's life. I grieved over the loss of his life but did not understand the depth of the trauma my Black family members were experiencing.

My white world, my white experience, had whitewashed the real history that Black families in this nation had experienced when it came to police mistreatment and abuse. With no true history, a history that most white people don't want to hear, there can't be real context to what was going on. My experience in the church is that some white Christians don't want to know the real history. Could it be that it's just too painful, fosters too much guilt and shame that even though it could help us understand the repair that is needed, they don't want to hear it?

Some have accused me that bringing up history is divisive and racist in itself. These accusers have left the church, unfriended me on social media, said nasty things about my attempts to shed some light. I guess as humans, it's just easier for some to sweep things under the rug and pretend like it doesn't exist, but it doesn't help. It's like putting a clean diaper over a dirty diaper on a baby. How well does that work?

On April 11, 2012, George Zimmerman was charged with 2nd-degree murder, and things seemingly settled down. I felt like I wouldn't have to say anything. Some would say, "why would you even worry about this? Your job is to preach the Gospel, leave it alone." That's like saying you just ignore all that your church family is going thru and just preach the gospel. My family had become diverse, and it was no longer an option.

I wasn't saying anything, but it wasn't right. It was so wrong. In all actuality, we were missing some real bridge-building opportunities.

On July 13, 2013, a jury acquitted George Zimmerman of the murder charges. Even though most of the protests in our nation were peaceful, it was back in our lives. We had a few discussions around this in our staff meeting, probably because, for whatever reason, we were being influenced by the polarization that was taking place in our nation and churches. If truth be told, we were probably all afraid to say something that would cause more harm, and so we remained silent. This is after twenty years of being together. How sad is that? We had no idea how to have a conversation about these issues that were so dramatically affecting us. We still had no idea about each other's lives and how even to begin these conversations that needed to happen. So much for let's just love Jesus and move on. Our fear paralyzed us and kept us from offering some of the necessary biblical expressions. There was no lament, no compassion, grace, or mercy offered in the church. We just avoided each other. How sad is that?

On August 9, 2014, it happened again. A 28-year-old police officer by the name of Darren Wilson fatally shot Michael Brown in Ferguson, Missouri, a suburb of St. Louis. By November of that year, a grand jury had decided not to indict the officer. This time the events ignited tremendous unrest in Ferguson that we witnessed every single day in the news.

Singular events like this have a way of igniting emotions on both sides of the audience. Most white people will always try and find excuses for something like this happening. It's almost like we are trying to find ways to defend our whiteness without even realizing that's what we are doing. Most people of color will see it as a continued onslaught of violence against young

Black men. They find themselves dealing with the pain of racial trauma that just won't go away. Black Lives Matter had now come to the forefront of Black people saying enough was enough. Right away, white people started getting defensive about that. Well, don't all lives matter?

The absurdity of that question is obvious. Of course, all lives matter. But at this point in our history, it was coming to light that so many young men had died and were dying as a result of police violence. History showed this to be accurate, and when Black people wanted to raise their voices, even white people in the church began to raise voices of opposition.

Somehow, we have to lift our eyes to the bigger picture of what is happening because of these events. Historical context must come into play when these events take place. If we continue to avoid it, we will never know the truth and never be free of our impotence to do anything about fostering healing along these racial lines. We will never be able to build healing bridges into each other's lives. We will never be motivated to offer lament and grace-filled comfort to our families of color that are so suffering in the bowels of racial trauma. If anyone should understand how the truth can set you free, it should be us, the children of God. But we continue to settle for less. But this wouldn't be the first time that the church has been caught bringing up the rear.

Luke 16:8 (KJV)

[8] And the lord commended the unjust steward because he had done wisely: for the children of this world are in their generation wiser than the children of light.

There are so many people involved in the hard work of love, a love that would bring justice to so many people. People have been harmed by not only the interpersonal acts of racism but also the systems of racism. Systems that have done nothing but benefit white people and marginalize people of color, purposefully hold them back from the privileges of those who hold the power to create said systems.

But I have to ask, where is the church?

Why are we continuing to stick our heads in the sand about these issues and purposefully excuse our lack of involvement?

It was about this time in my journey that I began to reach out to my daughter in law. Dr. Lucretia Carter Berry. She happens to be African American. She married our son Nathan and gave us three beautiful granddaughters. They were our youth pastors for five years in the early 2000s. They had moved back to North Carolina and were making their mark in the world there. Even though up to this point, our conversations around race had been minimal at best.

Anne and I had adopted two African American children, and of course, we leaned very heavily on her for help. But as I look back, it grieves me that we never went very deep in conversations with her, nor were we very sensitive about what it was like to marry into this predominantly white family.

At this point, we were probably still under the belief that if we don't see color, it's a good thing. I still believed that if we all just loved Jesus, everything would be ok. What a living example that became to me. How many years she was in our family and we didn't really see her, weren't motivated to really get to know her, understand her, where she came from and who she really was. I don't remember many times at all that I ever gave her space to share her experience, where I asked her to share her story. It doesn't matter if it's in your home, your workplace, your church, your community. This idea of color blindness, and that if we just love Jesus, everything will be ok, doesn't work. It's actually cruel, insensitive, and goes against so many biblical principles laid out to us in the laws of love.

My calls to her started out with my inabilities to make sense of these individual acts of racial injustices. I shared my anguish that I was voiceless and had no idea what to do as a Shepherd. While her mind was swimming in decades, even centuries of racial injustice, I was pressuring her for direction about what I should say or do about individual acts of violence. She was so kind and helpful to someone who, at the time, didn't have a clue about the bigger picture. Not once did I ask her how she was coping with all that was going on. Not once did I show her any care or concern as to how these events were impacting her. I'm sad to say I was just lost in my own issues.

It was during this time that she helped me craft a few statements, posted a couple of videos that I felt relieved me of my responsibility. I am so embarrassed to write some of these things, but this story is not just mine. It is the story of a lot of white Christians who can relate. My goal is to help us move forward and hopefully help you avoid some of my mistakes and insensitivity. My prayer is that we will be motivated to begin to work through anything that is standing in the way of us deeming this work as important. We have to open our hearts to the truth, gain context to the bigger picture. How can we offer anything to people who are hurting if we don't understand a more significant portion of what they have been through and what they are going through now?

The events kept coming. Events continued to happen that further drove us apart. People of color continued to suffer the cause and effects of both interpersonal and systemic racism. At the same time, it seemed white people grew more vocal about defending their whiteness and coming up with excuses for why there were so many young Black men ending up dead.

In our church, the silence was deafening.
Didn't we have anything to offer each other?

You wouldn't think so.

Then all of a sudden, it came home. On June 17th, 2015, the Charleston church massacre took place. Nine African American church members, including the senior pastor, were murdered in cold blood by Dylann Roof, a 21-year-old, who was a self-proclaimed white supremacist. He had entered the church, was welcomed, and attended the bible study before shooting the Pastor and his members. The Emanuel African Methodist Episcopal Church is one of the oldest Black churches in the United States. How could this happen? Better yet, why does this continue to happen? This single event motivated some steps within our nation to remove emblems associated with white supremacy. It even finally helped the South Carolina general assembly to find the courage to remove the Confederate Battle flag from the state capitol grounds.

Those long overdue positives aside, this event hit home, and I found myself back in Lucretia's face. I was hoping she could help me craft a statement, but this time it was different. I can't speak for her, but from my perspective, I was wearing her out. I was using her as a crutch. What was I thinking? This time I got a lot more than a statement.

I'm reminded of a time when Jesus encountered a blind man.

Mark 8:22-25 (NLT)

22 When they arrived at Bethsaida, some people brought a blind man to Jesus, and they begged him to touch the man and heal him. 23 Jesus took the blind man by the hand and led him out of the village. Then, spitting on the man's eyes, he laid his hands on him and asked, "Can you see anything now?"

24 The man looked around. "Yes," he said, "I see people, but I can't see them very clearly. They look like trees walking around."

25 Then Jesus placed his hands on the man's eyes again, and his eyes were opened. His sight was completely restored, and he could see everything clearly.

When it came to the calling on our lives to build bridges across ethnic and cultural divides, I was grateful that my eyes were beginning to open, that even though I couldn't see very clearly, at least I was beginning to see. Humans maybe looked like trees walking around, but my eyes were beginning to open, and I also realized that Jesus was not done helping me see more clearly.

7

Seeing More Clearly...

For almost forty years of being the Pastor of two great churches, it has been my heart to help people see more clearly. Help them see how much God loves them and wants a relationship with them. How much he wants to help them in every area of their lives. How much He wants to use them. Have them be a part of what He is doing in the earth. How much He needs us to help Him bring about His will in the earth. I know that sounds like a lot, but wow, what an opportunity.

I have declared what caused me to fall in love with God was how He cared about every area of our lives. How He loves everyone and wants to restore, redeem, and be intricately involved in our lives.

The uphill battle with this has always been that things don't always work out the way we want. Bad things still happen to good people. Jesus told us that there was a thief who wanted to do nothing but steal, kill, and destroy any good thing God desired for us. The thief's opposition made it difficult for people to buy into the fact that God wanted to do in their lives. It was difficult for them to see His will for their lives clearly.

I loved to teach people about the practicality of the Bible. I loved to teach that promises from God cover every area of our lives. Spiritually, mentally, physically, socially, economically, relationally, any area. Much of my teaching centered around helping people to have faith, develop trust in all that God wanted to do in them. I came to understand that we all came into this life with a purpose, a destiny, and if we could hook up with God's plans for our lives, our lives would have so much more meaning. We would experience so much more fulfillment hooked up with God. Our passion for helping people experience a personal relationship with Christ and learn how to live their lives for Him drove us.

I loved to teach people how I believed they could prosper in every area of their lives. You just learn how to believe God, trust Him, and your life will go places you never dreamed. After all, we are His representatives on the earth, and we need to represent well. We need to attain certain things and certain levels of success before we could do that. For a long time, I did a pretty good job helping people become self-absorbed with themselves and their drive for success. Later on, we found out that it didn't work as we presented it, and as people became frustrated and disillusioned by their lack of results, we began to lose them. We believed that if we could get people to open their hearts to Christ and teach them a little about faith, everything else would work out.

> *What I didn't see as clearly was that once we*
> *came into this incredible relationship with Jesus,*
> *our responsibility to reach others*
> *was foremost on His mind.*

Once we experienced the relationship that Jesus made available to us, it was our responsibility to help everyone on the planet to get in on it. After all, there is Jesus and the rest of us.

I am again reminded of the Blind man who had heard about Jesus.

Mark 8:22-25 (NLT)

22 When they arrived at Bethsaida, some people brought a blind man to Jesus, and they begged him to touch the man and heal him. 23 Jesus took the blind man by the hand and led him out of the village. Then, spitting on the man's eyes, he laid his hands on him and asked, "Can you see anything now?"

24 The man looked around. "Yes," he said, "I see people, but I can't see them very clearly. They look like trees walking around."

25 Then Jesus placed his hands on the man's eyes again, and his eyes were opened. His sight was completely restored, and he could see everything clearly.

This man's healing was progressive. When Jesus first touched his life, he began to see, but not well. Isn't it interesting how he could see people, but not clearly? But Jesus didn't leave him there, he touched him again, and everything cleared up. As I have thought about this account and my journey with God, most of my understanding of the things God was trying to show me came that way.

Whenever I thought I could see it all right away, I was usually missing something important. Whenever I thought I knew everything about anything, I often found out that there was a lot more to learn. The more dogmatic I became about something, the less clearly I could see.

Through almost forty years of pastoring, I told people that if you want to be a leader, you need to be leadable. If you want to be a teacher, you need to be teachable. If you are not leadable, you will not be a good leader. Also, if you are not teachable, you will not be an effective teacher.

---

*Does not scripture teach us to be quick to listen
and slow to speak?*

James 1:19 (NLT)

[19] Understand this, my dear brothers and sisters:
You must all be quick to listen, slow to speak,
and slow to get angry.

When it comes to Racism, talking about Racism, either people want to stick their heads in the sand and not say anything about it or everyone has an opinion and in specific environments are not afraid to share them. The reason these conversations, even in the Church, do not go well is that most people do not know what they are talking about. Because there has not been any truthful learning, most only speak out of what they "think" they know.

Some speak out of political dogma that is almost always divisive. You can't use political platforms to speak to these issues. You will only get into destructive arguments. Some try to speak out of a skewed false historical narrative. The history that we have learned leans heavily towards European conquests, colonization, and contributions.

Lastly, others just want to take the color-blind approach because they don't want to talk at all. The color-blind idea is the biggest stick your head in the sand approach. We won't get anywhere near healing if we embrace any of the approaches mentioned above.

You can always tell when no one knows what they are talking about because conversations like this tend to escalate very quickly into nothing more than arguments. We need Jesus to put his hands on our eyes again, help us clear up some things.

After the Charleston shootings, I went back to Lucretia for more help, help to craft another statement, but this time I got more than a statement.

She sent me a copy of "Dear White Christians: For Those Still Longing for Racial Reconciliation" authored by Dr. Jennifer Harvey,[6] who happened to be the associate professor of Religion right in Des Moines at Drake University.

This book was the answer to my prayers. It was the catalyst for my clearer vision. It connected me to the missing piece in our church. After twenty plus years of pastoring diversity and not really experiencing any true racial healing, this book was what opened my eyes, again.

The crazy part is that I almost missed the help.

When I received the book, I googled Dr. Harvey and learned that she was a gay ordained minister. I am ashamed of this, but my initial reaction was, "I can't read this book." I am assuming that a lot of you reading this book would have the same reaction. People (in my mind) in our church would not receive her or her insight. It seems that a lot of conservative evangelicals have reserved a particular place of disdain for people who are a part of the LBGTQ community. Most of us who are evangelical have judged that anyone who is a part of that community has nothing helpful to say to us.

While I was glancing back and forth to my computer screen reading about some of her theology and looking at her book, I heard the Holy Spirit say in my heart:

"Read the book."

I don't say that the Lord told me to do this or that very often, but here I heard the Lord tell me to do something that in my head I didn't want to do. "Read the book."

I remember asking my wife Anne, what should I do with this, and in her consistent wisdom, she said, "Read the book."

Having to lay aside my bias, my bigotry, and outright judgment of her, I started reading "Dear White Christians."

I had been praying about my frustration with how we were stuck in the reconciliation process — twenty plus years of loving each other, doing church together, yet more divided than ever.

I was asking for answers, and when they came, I almost didn't dare to open my heart to it. Almost from the opening chapter, her words challenged the validity of the Reconciliation

Paradigm. How all we needed to do was love each other and open our hearts to each other and love Jesus, and everything would work out the way it was supposed to. She declared that by itself, it did not work. She walked me through case after case historically and how it continued to come up short and fail miserably by itself. As I was reading, I felt myself getting defensive, somewhat angry, and thinking, she hasn't' seen what's going on in our church. But then I would remember, but what's going on in our church isn't working, and I would continue reading. It's one thing to bring people from different ethnicities and cultures together. Still, it's another thing to do the work of really getting to know each other, listening, and learning from one another about each other's experience.

I'm reminded of something Peter said in his letter,

1 Peter 3:7 (KJV)

[7] Likewise, ye husbands, dwell with them according to knowledge, giving honour unto the wife, as unto the weaker vessel, and as being heirs together of the grace of life; that your prayers be not hindered.

Peter tells husbands about their responsibility to learn about their wives, to learn about how they think, what's important to them and what's not. The implication here is that if you want to have any meaningful relationship, you must listen to her and learn. He implies that her experience is not yours, and you need to learn about her experience, and when you do, things are going to be better.

In my relationship with Anne, whenever she would try and open up with me and be truthful about her feelings, I would just try and fix her or her situation, not really understanding what she was going through. More than once, I would hear her say, "I don't want you to fix me. I just want you to *listen* to me." I want you to *hear* me.

She was looking for empathy, someone she could talk to, for someone to at least make an effort to listen and try and understand what she was going through. When it comes to building relationships across ethnic lines, we could learn a lot right here. Most white people could take this advice in their relationships with people of color. Dwell with our brother and sisters of color according to knowledge.

That begins by listening and learning. The problem is that we don't usually want to do either. When it comes to racial disparity, we just want to spout off our opinions about what we think should be done or not done. Instead of listening and learning, we have formulated opinions in our minds (even if we never say them) of what people of color should think about these issues without any real knowledge of what they are going through.

Peter was in no way saying that wives were weaker than men in any way other than maybe physically. Nor am I implying that people of color are weaker than white people in any way, shape, or form. I am saying that their experience has been different. White supremacy and privilege have been a power structure that has disenfranchised people of color from the same benefits of white people. If their experience has not been ours, how can we really speak to them about what they should do or not do? How can we judge what they say or don't say with no context to their journey?

As I have navigated this cross-cultural journey, I have watched how, whenever it comes to gaining some knowledge about what people of color have gone through and experienced at the hands of the majority culture, people get very defensive.

Most people believe that because they didn't own slaves or haven't committed any outward racist behavior, have friends of color, or claim to be color blind that they shouldn't have to have these conversations. I have heard that it shouldn't be a part of our discussions, especially in the church and that we should just all love Jesus and move on.

I have been told that having these conversations, to bring anything up about the past, is racist and divisive in itself. I wonder what kind of relationship a husband would have with his wife if all he ever told her was that she needed to get over whatever she was dealing with and move on. Just trust Jesus. He may be a good husband in some ways, but if he doesn't learn to listen and understand her, things are not going to end well.

As white people, we need to quit making this about us. We need to understand that no one is trying to make you out to be an evil or racist person. I realize that these conversations are uncomfortable and can foster feelings of shame and guilt. But the truth is it's not about you. It's about what our family of color has faced their whole lives and what they still face in this so-called better world. We have to quit dismissing people's pain by telling them they just need to get over it.

Interpersonal racism may be less common today, maybe not, but have you ever learned about the construct of racism? Have you ever learned about the systemic elements of racism that our brothers and sisters face every day of their lives? There are systems put in place that have marginalized them and disenfranchised them from many of the opportunities that we, as white people, have enjoyed all of our lives.

Overt acts of racism still exist. I think we all know this. What a huge burden it is upon their lives. But another element of this burden that weighs heavily on them are the systems that have been put in place to make life harder for them.

What am I saying? If you and I continue to avoid our history, the real history, how can we have any context to what is really going on in their lives? If you don't learn about what they have faced and have endured at the hands of the majority culture, how can you have any real context? How can you understand? And if you don't understand, how can there be healing? We won't have the heart to work on the repair that is needed to foster true healing if we avoid the historical facts of systemic racism.

We won't understand the biblical responsibility. We have to do the hard work of love and be anti-racist and help make right all the wrongs that have occurred.

As followers of Christ: we must be the voice and labor of this repair, but if you won't open up your heart to what has happened, how can we?

If we ignore 246 years of slavery, 100 years of Jim Crow laws, laws that were a collection of state and local statutes that legalized racial segregation. These laws existed for about 100 years, from the post-civil war era until 1968. Laws that were meant to marginalize African Americans by denying them the right to vote, hold jobs, get an education, and a lot of other opportunities. Those who attempted to defy the Jim Crow laws often faced arrest, fines, jail time, violence, and death.

If we ignore two decades of resistance of the civil rights movement, the new Jim Crow, systemic racial injustice in the criminal system, economics, education, housing, and politics, how can we bring help to the table?

It's just easier to deny our culpability and responsibility to do anything about this.

When Christians attack this work, dismiss it as something other than our responsibility as followers of Christ, it grieves my heart. I have been told that I need just to preach Christ, and everything will work out. In other words, leave this alone.

My son Nathan Berry made a statement that resounded with me.

"This "Jesus is the only Answer" is a classic cop-out and is a part of many people's journey into American life outside of their own. *For me, this is the definition of using the Lord's name in vain.* Using Jesus' name as a weapon to degrade the heart, and very hard work of another person is never ok. This idea is kin to Christians using Jesus' name in the origins of race/ism in America and its church. People are exposing that they believe racism is not systemic but rather a soft issue that can be resolved through friendships and probably an ethnic dinner or two."

If you have ever been someone who dismissed this work by claiming that preaching Jesus was all we needed to do, please consider that our responsibility goes well beyond that statement.

Systemic racism is still a problem that people of color deal with daily.

I am reminded of the encounter Jesus had with Zacchaeus. Jesus changed this man's life, and a big part of the change manifested this way.

Luke 19:8 (NLT)

8 Meanwhile, Zacchaeus stood before the Lord and said, "I will give half my wealth to the poor, Lord, and if I have cheated people on their taxes, I will give them back four times as much!"

He could have put all that cheating under the blood, but instead, he committed to repair the damage he had done and look at Jesus' response to him.

Luke 19:9 (NLT)

9 Jesus responded, "Salvation has come to this home today, for this man has shown himself to be a true son of Abraham.

Zacchaeus's commitment to repair is what Jesus responded to. I wonder what would happen if we got off of our Political high horses and got on a Christian donkey with this biblical attitude.

Isaiah 58:12 (MSG)

9-12 "If you get rid of unfair practices,
quit blaming victims,
quit gossiping about other people's sins,
If you are generous with the hungry
and start giving yourselves to the down-and-out,
Your lives will begin to glow in the darkness,
your shadowed lives will be bathed in sunlight.
I will always show you where to go.
I'll give you a full life in the emptiest of

places—
firm muscles, strong bones.
You'll be like a well-watered garden,
a gurgling spring that never runs dry.
You'll use the old rubble of past lives
to build a new,
rebuild the foundations from out of your past.
You'll be known as those who can fix anything,
restore old ruins, rebuild and renovate,
make the community livable again.

Can there be any reconciliation without repair? Dr. Jennifer Harvey's research and writing opened my mind and heart in so many ways. She helped me see what we were missing, led us into the next steps that have launched us into more profound and meaningful relationships. She challenged us to find the courage to get in the trenches of what we call bridge building. She helped us do more than just talking about building bridges but do it.

To think that I almost did not read her book. My bigotry could have kept me from receiving the help I needed to navigate the next steps. That I could have missed out on the friendship that we have since developed. I am and always will be eternally grateful for her and her passion for racial justice and anti-racism work. For all the help she has been to me in this journey.

8

Finding My Voice...

Anne and I have raised eight children. As a parent, I remember how exciting it was when each one of the children spoke their first words. I was so excited whether it was Mommy, Daddy, or something else. It meant things were about to change.

For so long in their infancy, they couldn't articulate to you their feelings, good or bad. Not knowing what a baby needs can be frustrating, to say the least. I know that mothers have this innate ability to discern baby's needs even without words, but you have to admit that when our children can articulate what they want, it's a relief.

At this point in the journey, I began to find my voice. It may have only been a few words in the beginning, and even though I may have struggled to voice those few words to the family at Cornerstone, they were words. I was learning so much about the divisions and why the 11 o'clock hour on Sunday mornings had become the most segregated hour. I was beginning to understand the construct of race, how it was created, and what it did to damage my family of color.

With knowledge comes responsibility, and my first responsibility was to give voice to the truth.

I needed to tell the truth about was needed to help us begin to build bridges across the sacred divides that had kept us separated in the body of Christ.

One of the first things we did was commit to telling the truth. To share with our family how important it was to learn the truth. We had always taught that it was the truth that would set us free, but I guess in this area, it was believed that the best thing we could do was avoid the truth, but not anymore.

Lucretia, whom I had leaned on for my voice, had been navigating her personal journey and decided to engage in truth-telling also.

With a background in education, curriculum, and instruction, she decided to develop a curriculum to help people learn some truth that would help them take the first steps towards racial healing. She realized that for us to have healthy conversations around race and racism in our homes, churches, and communities, we needed to move beyond our empty opinions and be empowered by education. She understood our need for language, history, and context. After all, how could we ever hope to dismantle racism without informed conversations? She desired to help us take a look at the history of our nation and discover how race has influenced how we live, where we live and whom we live with.

Her heart was to create a study where you wouldn't feel judged or victimized. She wanted to help us move our conversations beyond empty opinion and individual experiences. To help us gain the resolve to engage in racial healing and anti-racism work.

Dr. Lucretia Carter Berry's curriculum is called "*What Lies Between Us.*"[7] She developed this curriculum with a Journal and Guide that fulfills every goal mentioned above.

For more information about the curriculum, check out brownicity.com.

I have taken the study myself and discovered the power of understanding. We decided to host a "What Lies Between Us" seminar here at Cornerstone Family Church. In the beginning, it was all the voice I had. I shared about the books I was reading and what I was learning and how I felt that God had shown me what some of the next steps were. After all, we were a church committed to building bridges across the racial divide in the body of Christ. Or were we?

When you find your voice and start using it, some are going to be excited, and some are going to wish you had just kept your mouth shut. It is unavoidable, so you have to decide why you are doing this. The how is important, but if you don't know the why, the how won't matter because you won't last. This work of love is not for the faint at heart. I wish I could tell you that whenever you do what it is that God is leading you into that everything will just come together. The truth, many times you do what God tells you, there will be significant opposition. Bridge Building work challenges the very strongholds the enemy has used to keep us divided from the beginning of time. Don't ever think that the devil is going just to roll over and let you bring healing to the racial divides he used us to create. But in the same breath, I have to tell you that whatever is born of God will overcome if you give it time and faith.

In our first group study, we had over 300 people sign up to take it. We were so excited, because amid a few more people walking away, over 300 people signed up to take this course. We had Blacks, whites, Hispanic, and Asian people sign up for the course. Following the instructions in Lucretia's Journal and Guide, we watched the documentary *"Race the Power of Illusion."*[8] The first weeks of the study, we weren't allowed to have any discussion. It was all about learning. There would be time for discussion later after we had all completed the learning part of the study.

We wanted to move beyond the empty opinions that fueled most of the conversations up to this point. It was crazy what we learned. So much about race was coming to light. We learned that race was not biological. We learned that race was created, was a social, economic construct created to marginalize people of color and benefit white people. We learned how it was embedded in our government, in our educational institutions, into our laws. We learned what White Supremacy and Privilege were. After each video, we would allow people to share what they were learning from the videos. Only what they were learning, not what they thought about the content.

It was eye-opening how little the white people knew about the systemic elements of racism.

People would share what they learned, and then they would want to follow up with I'm so sorry, I just didn't know. You could feel the tension in our diverse group beginning to mount. When white people would express that systemic racism was not even on their radar, they didn't even know that it existed, that an unfair disadvantage to people of color, some people of color began to voice frustration and anger about those statements. "How could you not know about these systems that have benefited you all the while holding us back, holding us down and doing nothing but making our lives harder."

Now we had all this guilt, shame, and anger manifesting in the middle of this study. Some could have thought that this was the end of any meaningful conclusion. The opposite is true. What you have to embrace is that because this thing is of God and we were called to this reconciliation work, we had no choice but to lean into each other and allow grace and love to do its work.

Finally, it came time to enter into the discussion phase of the study, so we decided to break up into small groups to have our discussions. On the first night of the discussions, we were down 100 people. There were Black and white people who decided that they wanted nothing to do with the discussion elements of this study. Shame, guilt, and anger were winning out. I'm not saying they all left the church; they just didn't come back to the study. The good news is that we still had 200 people engaged, learning, and growing in their bridge-building capabilities.

This study was a game-changer for us. It moved us. It helped us take baby steps toward actually being a part of racial healing. It introduced us to so many things. As white people, we had to embrace all the shame and guilt that comes along with the light that was shed on our history and experience. We discovered the importance of empathy in this process. People of color had to be willing to allow the anger from racial trauma in their lives to be healed. They had to open their hearts to their white brothers and sisters and forgive. Isn't it amazing how we can live with each other and avoid conversations around things we resent about each other? Sometimes we just box things up and believe that avoiding any conversation about the things in the box will help us tolerate each other.

By the time the study finished, we had about half of those who had started. I was a little discouraged by that. But in the end, we had a new remnant of people committed and engaged in doing the hard work of love.

No sooner than we finished, people wanted to know what was next. What can we do, what do we need to do next was the question of the hour? I get that, and we began to challenge people to continue their learning, but also to follow their passions and find ways to get involved in advocating for their brothers and sisters of color. One thing I want to mention here is that something that might be a better question to ask is, "Why?" If you don't know why this work is essential, if you don't understand this is the gospel, you won't last. The work is enormous, but the reality is that because we created the construct of race, we can dismantle it. But if you don't know why this work is so important, if you don't understand that it is part of the gospel work, we have been called to, when it gets hard, you will walk away.

It's part of white privilege, you don't have to do this work, you can walk away at any moment, and your life won't be impacted. But if there is one thing that I have learned that people of color want more than our apologies is for us not to quit, to stay engaged. To do the anti-racist work that is necessary to get these systems that we created off their backs.

Seeing Race for what it is.

Having had the opportunity over almost 40 years of pastoring to travel the world and experience so many different ethnic and cultural groups of people, one of the main things I would always walk away with is that people are people. It didn't matter what your skin tone was, what your culture was, what kind of clothes you wore or didn't wear, what your language was, people are people. Our issues are all the same; our hopes and dreams are all the same, our fears and the things that concern us are all the same.

We are all human; we are God's creation and are all made in the likeness and image of Him. Genesis 1: 26

All of our lives, we've learned race to be biological, that it's about skin tone, the texture of hair, size of our noses and ears. These biological differences were used in the infant stages of our nation to justify different treatment of people based on the color of their skin and the texture of their hair. This race belief led to a narrative that began to take hold within the ranks of those embedded in the power structures of this budding new nation, white European men. Somehow the abuse and enslavement of people of color had to be justified by these founders. They turned to the scientific community of their time and asked for their help in proving their narrative. They asked for help in proving that their Black slaves were somehow less than human, that because they were less than human, they were not eligible for any of the new rights and freedoms founded within this new nation.

It never happened. Race was never proven to be biological, but it didn't stop the narrative that race was biological and that not all human beings had to be treated equally. The belief that race was biological fueled the narrative of racial difference and led to the human-made construct of race and racism. Because we had different hues of skin, different textures of hair, and other surface differences, it was decided that other human beings could be classified and treated differently than their white European counterparts.

Where was the Church? Where were those who understood and believed in the sanctity of the scripture? Where was their voice of opposition to this narrative? To the injustices that led to 246 years of slavery. Had the story of racial difference so blinded them that they just sat in the shadows with no voice? To imply that everyone sat idly by while this narrative continued to grow would be a little disingenuous, but too many said nothing. Many chimed in with the narrative, offering skewed biblical interpretation to justify the construct.

Even after a civil war and the emancipation of slaves, the narrative continued, which led to 100 years of Jim Crow laws that continued to misuse and abuse people of color solely based on the color of their skin.

Early in the history of our nation, churches began to succumb to the pressures of the narrative and started to treat members differently in their houses of worship. Different rules were established for the Black members to appease white members. When they could pray, approach the altar, where and when they could serve. It wasn't long, and they began to feel like second class citizens in their own houses of worship.

Because White leaders in the church could not find their voice of opposition to the narrative, it continued to grow and took over their own houses of worship. This situation led to Black members saying enough is enough. "If we can't be treated as the children of God we are, and if you can't treat us with the dignity and respect we deserve, we will leave."

Can you imagine the pain of being treated so disrespectfully by leaders in your church? Can you imagine not being able to pray with other white members, not being able to approach the alters when other white members were there, having to sit in the back or up in a balcony because of internal segregation, all because of the color of your skin.

I put a post on Facebook that the only reason we have a segregated church today is because of racism in the white church, and boy did I ignite a firestorm of criticism. Even though it was historically and factually accurate, so many got nasty and labeled me a racist myself just for bringing it up.

I am convinced that the Church is still the most segregated entity in America today, not because of demographics, but rather because we continue to allow the narrative of racial difference to fuel our biases and keep us from speaking up about all of the wrongs that continue to exist in the church world today. We still believe, even though we may never give voice to this, we know how to do church better. We brag that we are welcoming to everyone but refuse to open ourselves up to the diversity of thought and expression.

When churches begin to diversify in their pews, sometimes the diversity in leadership or staff doesn't change to reflect the people they are serving. So again, you have white church members deciding about how everything is going to run with little consideration to the members of color and their needs.

At some point in time, you will have to lay down your fear of chasing all your white members off.

You will have to realize that if God is in this (and how could he not be), it will work out.

At some point in time, you will have to realize that preaching Jesus is not your only responsibility to the church you pastor or attend. You will have to recognize that your whole life, you have been marinating in a society that perpetuates the narrative that white is better. Even if you won't give mental assent to that, it's what you have been exposed to all your life.

It's in our criminal justice system, our education system, our housing policies, and even in political structures. These systems still permeate our society today and negatively affect our brothers and sisters of color. We cannot stay in the shadows and not do something about it. Just because it doesn't impact us directly, we cannot remain silent.

If there is one thing that Jesus exemplified to us as Christians, it's that he bypassed our entire religious order to go to the people who had been pushed out of the conduits of opportunity. They were pushed out by constructs that were created by those in power. He spoke against the systems and empathized with the disenfranchised people.

Ignoring the issues that plague our family members of color because they don't overtly affect our lives is precisely why we are still predominately segregated. It seems that when you begin to give voice to these injustices, white Christians want to push back and stick their heads in the sand and declare that these issues are divisive and should not be brought into the church, all the while the people we claim to love like ourselves are suffering.

Some have used the excuse that because their churches are all or (predominantly white), that it's never an issue as if having no people of color in their congregations absolves them of this responsibility. The narrative of racial difference and the biases that it creates are still alive today. I know we want to think all things are different now, but the truth is that the systems still exist. Because white people constructed them, it will take us playing a significant role in their deconstruction. If we don't raise our voice and get involved, it won't happen.

As the church, we are supposed to come out from under our bushels and let our light shine. We are way overdue in our activism. It's not like we have never done this before. Look at how many people are passionate about fighting against sex-trafficking in our nation today. We hear all day long about how organizations are actively speaking up and getting involved as it relates to human rights violations in other nations.

In this nation, we tend just to blame people who are suffering, like it's their fault somehow. After all, this is the United States, where everyone has the same opportunities. We have all had hardships, but only people of color have had to face feeling second class in just about every area of our society because of the color of their skin.

The systems are real and still exist today to give white people the advantage and put people of color at a disadvantage.

I have to admit that sometimes I am bewildered by the lack of empathy, the lack of compassion for Christians when it comes to these issues. Maybe it's not so much about the hardness of someone's heart as it is that many people just don't know where to start. I have to believe that if we don't ignore the Holy Spirit that lives in us, He will show us steps. Perhaps one of your first steps was reading this book. With me, it all came to life with a book. Maybe it's the same for you now.

Jesus prayed an amazing prayer right before he left us by ascending to the Father in John 17.

John 17:20-21 (NLT)

20 "I am praying not only for these disciples but also for all who will ever believe in me through their message. 21 I pray that they will all be one, just as you and I are one—as you are in me, Father, and I am in you. And may they be in us so that the world will believe you sent me.

Remember, this is the last recorded prayer right before he left, so I know that its important and worthy of reflection. In the prayer, he said he wasn't just praying for those who were there at the time but also for those who would come to believe in Him. Let's read.

I have to believe that he prayed this prayer because he knew what was coming. Because he knew the enemy would do everything he could to divide and conquer us. From Cain and Abel, he was working tirelessly to keep us at odds with each other. After centuries of division, Jesus comes on the scene and wants to disrupt the strongholds of divisiveness and bring healing. The only problem is that he needs us to do our part. So, the prayer gives me hope. It energizes me to be an active part of disrupting the enemies work. With the Holy Spirit in us, we can do this. We can choose to let the Holy Spirit empower and guide us as we make this a part of our work to repair. All of this is so that the world, those on the outside of a relationship with Christ, would be so captivated by our love for one another that they would give us a real opportunity to share the love of Jesus with them.

When we started Cornerstone in 1991, this prayer would not go away. Every time we would think about our new "work," this prayer would come into my heart. Even with limited understanding about where it was going to lead us, it became the verse that drove us into the desire to build bridges across the sacred divides that had kept us apart.

Anne and I embraced this call. Along the way, whenever new understanding would come, and the cost was made known we kept saying yes. Here we are, Lord, please send us. It's our prayer that you will join the cause and become a part of bringing this healing to the most segregated hour.

9

What Does Love Require...

A lot!

We have taught the Bible for over 40 years now, and I have to say that it amazes me how easy it is to drift so far from the ministry priorities that Jesus walked out for us.

In the Zacchaeus story, Jesus told everyone that he came to seek and save the lost. In evangelical circles, we have shrink-wrapped that statement into a package that, when opened, reveals that our assumed only responsibility is to share Jesus with people and help them experience his love in their lives.

We will go on to teach people how to live for him, based on our system of beliefs and tell them if they develop their faith in our interpretations of scripture, everything in their lives will work out.

When it wasn't working out, and people looked for help, we would just tell them to keep working on their faith, and things would get better. If it didn't work out, many times, we would just deem them faithless, and in many cases, judge them at some level that they must be doing something wrong. We would then move on to those who seemed on the surface were making our interpretation of scripture work.

The belief that we had the corner on the interpretation of scripture was paramount. When you think you have the correct interpretation of scripture, it's easy to become dogmatic about snippets of scripture. It's easy to become prideful and condescending towards others who don't agree with you. If you are not careful, you will begin to prioritize your dogma and isolate yourself around said dogma. One of the big problems with this is that your focus centers on it, and you become hardened towards other elements of the teachings of Jesus.

Paul told the church at Philippi how we, as followers of Christ, should live, do ministry, and how we should treat each other as the family of God.

Philippians 2:1-8 (NLT)

[1] Is there any encouragement from belonging to Christ? Any comfort from his love? Any fellowship together in the Spirit? Are your hearts tender and compassionate? [2] Then make me truly happy by agreeing wholeheartedly with each other, loving one another, and working together with one mind and purpose.

[3] Don't be selfish; don't try to impress others. Be humble, thinking of others as better than yourselves. [4] Don't look out only for your own interests, but take an interest in others, too.

[5] You must have the same attitude that Christ Jesus had. [6] Though he was God, he did not think of equality with God as something to cling to.

⁷ Instead, he gave up his divine privileges; he took the humble position of a slave and was born as a human being. When he appeared in human form, ⁸ he humbled himself in obedience to God and died a criminal's death on a cross.

It can't always be about us and how our lives are moving forward. Sometimes as Jesus said, we must die to ourselves for the benefit of others. We have to pick up our cross and follow Him. Where? To address the needs of those who have been rejected, judged, marginalized, and disenfranchised.

I remember early in our ministry I heard the Lord say,

"If you go after the people nobody wants, I will give you the people everyone is trying to get."

When I shared it, everyone loved the concept. Still, when we actually decided to do it and the people nobody wanted started coming to the church, people began second-guessing their support, and some even quit coming. I started hearing let's just go minister to those people but let's not bring them into our family. If it gets too messy, people will stop coming. Some might wonder how we could be true followers of Christ and have this self-preservation paradigm, but it happens all the time.

It's here that we have to justify our beliefs. It's here that we start coming up with all kinds of excuses why we aren't doing the work Jesus has called us to do. We have reasons for why we refuse to get our hands dirty.

The lyrics to the song "Will We Ever Rise" by The Brilliance⁹ are so powerful.

They read:

"Will we ever rise? Will we ever rise above the fear? Can we learn to see the need? Can we share humanity?

Will we ever rise above the hate? Can we learn another way? I can see another day come, broken people, we can be made whole, as we lay down our weapons, open up our hearts, love is breaking us, love is remaking us."

What Does Love Require? After walking out ministry for almost 40 years, I found myself asking and answering this question all over again. Did I know the answer to that question? Was I doing ministry out of that answer? I wasn't sure. Was I connected to the heart of Jesus; did I really understand what was important to Him?

I think it's necessary for all of us who are followers of Christ to ask ourselves this question, is what's important to Him vital to me?

Do you know what's important to Him, or have you lost sight of it? Sometimes I have gotten so busy trying to live up to unrealistic expectations and make my way in this life that I haven't given this question much thought.

We have learned that it's pretty easy to hide in our little religious circles, but in doing that, we will find ourselves on the outside looking in. We'll go to heaven, but we will also find ourselves a long way from where the heart of Jesus truly resides.

As I began to look at ministry in this new light, I realized that in almost 40 years of ministry, I had never preached a series on Justice. I'm not even sure if I grasped the true meaning of the word. I am not sure I grasped how important it actually is to God.

Psalms 37:28a

For the Lord loves justice

The parables of Jesus forced us to look at justice. I could say that Jesus made us look at what's important to him. Remember the Good Samaritan, the story of Zacchaeus. Do you remember when Jesus stood up in the temple and quoted Isaiah and the prophecy about himself?

Luke 4:18 New Living Translation (NLT)

18 "The Spirit of the Lord is upon me, for he has anointed me to bring Good News to the poor. He has sent me to proclaim that captives will be released, that the blind will see, that the oppressed will be set free,

All of these actions that He proclaimed revealed the work that you and I should be doing. They revealed to all of us what was important to Jesus and what wasn't. I love scripture. I love to wrestle with it. Here is my point: There are many beliefs and sermons I preached in the early years of my ministry that I have had to adjust.

Revelation and understanding are ongoing, and because we all are in a constant state of learning, it's dangerous to lock in on something and claim we have found the exact meaning. Many times we do this without the required context. Something Jesus said got me thinking. One day when the religious order of the day was trying to compromise His work, this discourse took place.

Matthew 22:34-40 (NLT)

[34] But when the Pharisees heard that he had silenced the Sadducees with his reply, they met together to question him again. [35] One of them, an expert in religious law, tried to trap him with this question: [36] "Teacher, which is the most important commandment in the law of Moses?"

[37] Jesus replied, "'You must love the Lord your God with all your heart, all your soul, and all your mind.' [38] This is the first and greatest commandment. [39] A second is equally important: 'Love your neighbor as yourself.' [40] The entire law and all the demands of the prophets are based on these two commandments."

Even after reading this scripture hundreds of times, I saw a couple of things that I had never seen before.

First, I saw that loving your neighbor as yourself was a commandment equally as important as the first, which was to love the Lord God with all your heart. Equally as important...that got my attention.

Second, Jesus said that the entire law and all the demands of the prophets are based on these two commandments.

Could it be that everything I believe about scripture has to filter through these two commandments, and if it doesn't pass through, my understanding might be wrong? It got me thinking and reflecting on what I was teaching and what I believed. I began to have uncomfortable feelings in my heart. I have to admit that it would have just been easier to ignore this conflict. After all, it's been 40 years, and if I have approached all that I believe without filtering it through these laws of love, what was I supposed to do?

Have you ever heard the phrase?

"Don't Bury Your Head in the Sand."

Early on, people believed that this phrase came from how an Ostrich, when threatened, would bury his head in the sand, thinking that if it couldn't see it's enemy, then it's enemy couldn't see it. It's not true, but because the Ostrich is not the smartest bird in the world, it got stuck with this stupid act.

Sometimes we use this phrase on each other because we feel like people we care about are ignoring essential issues in their lives. They are pretending that they don't exist, that if they deny them or ignore them, they will just go away. Our response to that is, "That's Stupid."

In the Church, we have gotten pretty good at ignoring justice and the work it requires, ignoring the real problems that Jesus has anointed us to work on.

I am not trying to be harsh but are we a church that has stuck our head in the sand instead of doing the real work we have been called to- helping people the way Jesus equipped us to. It will require us to get our heads out of the sand and get our hands dirty. It will require us to die to ourselves.

The problems of this world can be so overwhelming that sometimes it's just easier to ignore them, especially if they are not affecting our lives. Segregation in the body of Christ, injustices that exist to this day, injustices that impact our brothers and sisters of color can be so easily ignored because of segregation itself.

Some will claim that it doesn't affect them because there is no opportunity for diversity in their communities and churches.

That statement breaks my heart for several reasons. Can you really say that it seems you are saying that the pain people of color have and are experiencing in segregation is not your responsibility or concern as a Christ-follower?

Can I remind us all of a prayer that Jesus prayed right before he ascended to heaven? We call it His final prayer.

John 17 (NLT)

¹ After saying all these things, Jesus looked up to heaven and said, "Father, the hour has come. Glorify your Son so he can give glory back to you. ² For you have given him authority over everyone. He gives eternal life to each one you have given him. ³ And this is the way to have eternal life— (to clearly understand you), the only true God, and Jesus Christ.

⁶ "I have revealed you to the ones you gave me from this world. They were always yours. You gave them to me, and they have kept your word. ⁷ Now they know that everything I have is a gift from you, ⁸ for I have passed on to them the message you gave me. They accepted it and know that I came from you, and they believe you sent me.

¹¹ Now I am departing from the world; they are staying in this world, but I am coming to you. Holy Father, you have given me your name; *now protect them by the power of your name so that they will be united just as we are.*

20 "I am praying not only for these disciples but also for all who will ever believe in me through their message. **21** *I pray that they will all be one, just as you and I are one—as you are in me, Father, and I am in you. And may they be in us so that the world will believe you sent me.*

22 "I have given them the glory you gave me, (the power to do this) so they may be one as we are one. **23** I am in them and you are in me. *May they experience such perfect unity that the world will know that you sent me and that you love them as much as you love me*

I have asked myself over and over again, "Why did He pray this prayer?" Do you know why? Because He knew what was coming: Division and Divisiveness, a segregated body, a fractured body.

He didn't ignore it or pretend it wasn't going to happen. He didn't stick His head in the sand. He prayed for us.

He gave us His glory so that we would be emboldened, empowered, to work against forces that would divide us and be one. He didn't pray that we would ignore it, stick our head in the sand, and deny its effect on our lives.

Segregation runs deep in the Body of Christ.

We are still the most segregated hour in America.

It runs across ethnicity, culture, denominations, and generational lines, and a hundred other subcategories. Listen to something Paul said.

Galatians 3:26-29 (NLT)

[26] For you are all children of God through faith in Christ Jesus. [27] And all who have been united with Christ in baptism have put on Christ, like putting on new clothes.

[28] There is no longer Jew or Gentile, slave or free, male and female. For you are all one in Christ Jesus. [29] And now that you belong to Christ, you are the true children of Abraham. You are his heirs, and God's promise to Abraham belongs to you.

Paul is saying that all the barriers, all the walls that we built, all the things we used to divide ourselves are gone, all the old barriers are removed.

Remember, the churches at Galatia probably said. "Oh no, we just had a bunch of Jews here that told us if we really want to get close to God, we have to become like them, do things their way. Oh, there are still men and women; there is still slaves and free."

But Paul is trying to get them to "See…" See A New Reality. In Christ, there is no barriers, no big I's and little U's…there's Jesus and the rest of us. Talk about a new reality!

We, as the Church, have been commanded to usher in this new reality. As a follower of Jesus, it is our big responsibility to actively tear down these walls that divide us. We must actively stand against injustices even if we live, work, and worship in colorless spaces.

Dr. Martin Luther King Jr., in his letter from the Birmingham jail, wrote:

"Injustice anywhere is a threat to justice everywhere. We are caught in an inescapable network of mutuality, tied in a single garment of destiny. Whatever affects one directly, affects all indirectly."[10]

2 Corinthians 5:17-21 (VOICE)

[17] Therefore, if anyone is united with the Anointed One, that person is a new creation. The old life is gone—and see—a new life has begun! [18] All of this is *a gift* from *our Creator* God, who has *pursued us and* brought us into a restored *and healthy* relationship with Him through the Anointed. And He has given us *the same mission,* the ministry of reconciliation, *to bring others back to Him.* [19] *It is central to our good news that* God was in the Anointed making things right between Himself and the world. This means He does not hold their sins against them. But it also means He charges us to proclaim the message that heals and restores our broken relationships with God and each other.

For you and me to follow Jesus means that it is our responsibility to eliminate these constructed barriers that cause so much injustice and embrace the unity Jesus prayed for.

As a follower of Christ, we can't ignore these barriers that cause so much injustice. We must work to remove them, That We Will All Be One. Almost 30 years ago, Anne and I came to this city with a mandate, a calling. It's why we came.

Helping all people find and live their lives in Christ, bridging ethnic, cultural, denominational, and generational lines.

We believed that it would be our oneness that Jesus would be able to use to arrest the attention of the world.

Have you ever heard that the most segregated hour in America is the 11 o'clock church worship service hour? Martin Luther King Jr. is the one who said it…actually he said, "It is appalling that the most segregated hour in America is the 11 o'clock church service."[11]

It's not by accident that the Lord emphasized in our calling the ethnic and cultural divides that have plagued us for centuries. Barriers to unity were created to divide us and keep us divided. Fueled by racism, we still deal with these barriers. White churches justify it by saying, well, there's just more of us, or it's just demographics, or it's just how it is working out.

Red, Yellow, Black, and Brown churches could say, "man church is the only place we can get away from you and your superior attitudes and treatment." Even in our era of enlightenment, for the most part, we remain divided. We still allow barriers the enemy has constructed to keep us apart.

Even if we do come together like in many of our churches today, we really don't understand each other's experience of life. We don't know how to have constructive conversations about "Race" or "Racism."

Now I realize I have been doing this for a while, and this is where most white people start getting nervous and uncomfortable and maybe even a little mad. But I'm asking you not to quit reading. You're almost done. We cannot dismantle these barriers if we don't understand their construction. We can't stick our heads in the sand anymore.

2 Corinthians 2:11 (KJV)

¹¹ Lest Satan should get an advantage of us: for we are not ignorant of his devices.

One of the biggest lies the enemy has sold us is that if we don't talk about race, racism will end. Instead, our silence, our lack of education concerning his devices, pretending not to see color has left us impotent-unable to perform our responsibilities.

Let me ask you something.

Does not talking about cancer heal cancer? Does not talking about human trafficking end human trafficking? Bringing attention to a disease, whether personal or social, doesn't cause more suffering. Instead, spotlighting the problem mobilizes us toward ending the suffering. Studying the disease is what ultimately leads us to a cure.

¹¹ Lest Satan should get an advantage of us: for we are not ignorant of his devices.

We cannot hide behind the **Color-Blind Approach.** Many times, people with the best intentions default to "I don't see color." They believe that this will help. Well, first of all, it's a lie. We all see color, and it doesn't help. How can you deny someone's experience and be a part of the solution?

Most of the time, it is just people trying to say
they aren't racist.

Stay with me.

Others believe that talking about these issues is in itself racist. To speak about the past and all the wrong stirs up more hatred and division. Here's where I have had many people walk away from us and retreat into all white and Black spaces.

Why? Because this stuff is hard, but also because they believe in the "Jesus is the Only Answer" approach as the only safe way that we can do this. We just need to love one another. I only tell you these things to prepare you for the hard work that is ahead of you. We need you to engage in this justice work and not grow weary in your well-doing.

Ok, then let's go back to our question, "What does love require…?"

I believe that Jesus is the only answer, but for me to throw that on you with no concern about your experience, what you have been thru, without loving you enough to listen to you, try and understand where you've been and where you have come from, is kin to using the Lord's name in vain.

1 Peter 3:7 (KJV)

7 Likewise, ye husbands, dwell with them (Your Wife) according to knowledge, giving honor unto the wife

Peter said that if you want to have a meaningful relationship with your wife, you better educate yourself so you can understand her.

I don't know how good your relationship with your wife would be if you just told her to get over it and didn't offer any empathy.

We are at this place in our nation because we have refused to acknowledge the truth about what our brother and sisters of color have been thru and are still going thru. We're still divided and afraid to engage each other and talk about it. Therefore, we are still being taken advantage of by the enemies' devices.

Truth? What do we need to see?

Our country was built with systems of violent oppression. Near genocide of Native Americans. 265 Years of slavery that brought 4,000,000 Africans to this country against their will. One hundred years of Jim Crow laws that oppressed and marginalized Black and brown people even after slavery was abolished. Two Decades of resistance to Civil Rights.

The new Jim Crow, systemic racial injustice, injustice in our courts, economics, education, and housing policies. So, the question begs to be asked, what do we do? A better question is

"What does love require?"

We get our heads out of the sand, and we show some empathy.

In 44 years of marriage, I can't tell you how many times Anne has told me, "I don't want you to try and fix me, I just want you to listen." We embrace our call to reconcile. We open our hearts to listen, to learn, to be there for each other.

We quit acting like this work is not part of our Gospel mission. We ask the Lord to show us the ways we can get involved. We educate ourselves. We start a conversation born out of love and a desire to learn. We find someone open to being a part of this, and we say to each other I need you, you are my family, and I am tired of being divided.

I just want to be one of those people who, when God needs someone to do something, someone to help right a wrong, I want to have the courage to say,

"Lord, here I am, send me."

I don't have to have all the answers, just an open heart to do the real work Jesus wants me to do.

Observing our nation, with all the polarization and overwhelming divisiveness, could be so discouraging. Still, for me, the reality is that the darker it gets, the more opportunity we have to let our lights shine.

I sense that God is putting things in place to destroy all this darkness. He is raising a remnant of His kids who want to do something about this, who desire to be a part of the solution and will do the hard work of love to get God's will done in the earth.

Who will engage in real justice work for *all* people?

We are honored to be in this together.

A Final Prayer

Father, I thank you for revealing your heart to us. Thank you for helping us see how much you desire for us to be truly one. Forgive us for allowing so much division to develop in your body. Forgive us for not loving our neighbors as ourselves. Lord, as we move forward, I ask you to help us to see more clearly. To help us find the courage to be whom you created us to be. To love like you love. Lord, I ask you to show us our next steps, show us how we can be a repairer of the divisiveness that still exists among your children today. May we be a people of peace, with voices of hope, and willing to do the hard work of love. Amen

Brownicity:
Many Hues One Humanity

I am a part of an organization that I would like to recommend to you as you navigate this journey. Without Dr. Lucretia Carter Berry and Brownicity, I would not be where I am today.

www.brownicity.com

Brownicity

Pronounced like "ethnicity."

A combination of the words "Brown" and "Ethnicity" Brown represents melanin, the pigment we all have. Ethnicity means "that which we have in common." Essentially, we are all hues of brown.

Brownicity: Many Hues, One Humanity is a platform for disrupting the race narrative and its legacy of racism. They are family-focused and dedicated to advocacy, education, and support for racial healing and anti-racism.

Brownicity is encouraging, inspiring, helpful, and hopeful while promoting ONEness, healing ,and change. WE are proof that love defies race/isms! And we want to spread the LOVE!

Brownicity: Many Hues One Humanity

Bridge Building Solutions

If we have been a help and blessing to you through "Navigating Diversity in Our Most Segregated Hour," I invite you to continue the conversation by checking out our website and following us on Instagram and Facebook.

www.bridgebuildingsolutions.com
Facebook: Bridge Building Solutions
Instagram: Bridge Building Solutions
Email: dan@bridgebuildingsolutions.com

Bibliography

[1] Race Equity Institute. (2003). Foundations in Historical and Institutional Racism and Race – The Power of An Illusion. California Newsreel. www.racialequityinstitute.com

[2] Peterson, N. (2016). Emery University Columbia Theological Seminary.

[3] Tisby, J. (2019). The Color of Compromise.

[4] Gonzalez, J. (2004). United by Faith. Oxford University Press.

[5] Gonzalez, J. (2003). United by Faith. Oxford University Press.

[6] Harvey, J. (2014). Dear White Christians: For Those Still Longing for Racial Reconciliation. Eerdmans Publishing. Grand Rapids, MI.

[7] Berry, L. (2017). What Lies Between Us. Kindle.

[8] California Newsreel. (2003). Race the Power of an Illusion. Video.

[9] The Brilliance. (2017). Will We Ever Rise. Lyrics.

[10] King, M.L. Jr. (1963). Letter to Evangelical White Ministers. Birmingham, AL.

[11] King, M.L. Jr. (1960) Interview on Meet the Press Television.

Made in the USA
Coppell, TX
27 April 2020

21706456R00075